CUTTING UP IN THE KITCHEN

CUTTING UP

IN THE

KITCHEN

FOOD & FUN FROM
SOUTHERN NATIONAL'S CHEF

DUANE NUTTER

PHOTOGRAPHS BY DEBORAH WHITLAW LLEWELLYN

Gibbs Smith

First Edition
29 28 27 26 25   5 4 3 2 1

Published by
Gibbs Smith
570 N. Sportsplex Dr.
Kaysville, Utah 84037
1.800.835.4993 orders
www.gibbs-smith.com

Designed by Janice Shay and Sheryl Dickert
Production design by Renee Bond
Food styling by Annette Joseph
Printed and bound in China

Library of Congress Control Number: 2024942286
ISBN: 978-1-4236-6556-4
Ebook ISBN: 978-1-4236-6557-1

This product is made of FSC®-certified and other controlled material.

I dedicate this book to all the cooks in my life who instilled in me the joy of cooking for others. To my mother, Rosalind Russell-Nutter, who can make something out of nothing. You can taste the love she puts in every morsel that nourishes our hearts and souls. To my uncle Bob Russell, the quiet assassin on the barbecue pit, the meticulous fish-fryer, and the crackling boudin lover. Who could forget the first holiday feast I witnessed for a large group of people, all prepared by Janice and Earl Moon, some of the strongest cooks in our family? Cousin Janice made donuts, while Earl was making the gumbo and roasting a leg of lamb. I thought, at seven years old, I was in heaven! I was dipping homemade donuts in eggnog, sampling the ham, turkey, greens, sweet potatoes—you name it. Those two lovebirds could cook their asses off—RIP, cousin Earl.

One of my closest friends is Jared Bucci, and his mom, Sherry, makes lasagnas that are off the charts great. His aunt Susan Brady makes a cheesecake that is decadent beyond belief. My high school home economics teacher's first lesson was how to make butter from scratch, as well as homemade jam and scones. Linda Mortensen taught me all I needed to know about butter and delicious scones. Stan Hawley, a tough-as-nails, technically sound culinary instructor at South Seattle Community College, taught me the importance of research.

Lastly, my mentor, Chef Darryl Evans, converted all my love for food from family and friends into a profession that is equal parts artistry, economics, and personal pride for one's past and future. He used to say to me, "What's in the pot? Knowledge, if you look hard enough, big man."

CONTENTS

INTRODUCTION

Southerners are funny about their food, and I'm no exception. I remember my first "aha" moment like it was yesterday. Let me explain.

I was born in Morgan City, Louisiana, but when I was about seven years old my family moved to Seattle, Washington. I may have spent most of my childhood outside of the South, but we always ate Southern at home so I didn't know much about other foods. Drawn to cooking from a young age, I enrolled in the culinary program at South Seattle Community College and discovered a big world of food out there. My instructor taught French cooking techniques, and one day he explained how to make a classic coq au vin. I was on the edge of my seat, eagerly soaking in every word that poured out of his mouth.

Understand, I'm a 6-foot 5-inch Black man sporting some width on me—I don't look like your usual French chef. But I was awestruck by the mystique of French cuisine. I told myself, "I'm going to learn how to cook that fancy stuff, even if it is hard to pronounce." I couldn't wait to get out of class and tell my family and friends at the basketball court what I learned.

It was later that night, while studying my notes for the next morning's class, that I had the "aha" moment. I realized that when I got past the fancy French words and stripped the dish down to the technique of cooking it, coq au vin was basically what we Southerners called smothered chicken! The "aha" quickly became a "ha ha" moment. Food has kept me smiling ever since.

All of us have friends and family members who are adventurous eaters and some that just like to stay in their boxes. I remember going out to dinner with one of my not-so-adventurous friends. It is worth noting that two days prior we had enjoyed some jambalaya, which is a Southern Louisiana dish consisting of seafood, vegetables, and rice. On this night I ordered the paella—and I immediately got "the look" from my friend. I tried to explain that it was basically like the jambalaya we ate two nights ago, but the difference was in the spices—jambalaya is spiced with cayenne, paella with saffron. This night, I wanted to eat something less spicy.

"You chefs will eat anything," he grumbled.

It amazed me how this rice dish got my friend so worked up, but when I told him what was in the fried bologna sandwich he had ordered, that didn't bother him at all. It got me thinking, other than the familiar ingredients, why do we mainly like food that we know and feel comfortable eating?

Over the years, I have learned to take the best of regional and international cuisines and use them to make Southern food even better. Understand, I do enjoy traditional Southern foods, I just love expanding the possibilities of Southern cuisine. I think that the flavor combinations of the recipes I share here will resonate with savvy American eaters and home cooks who already enjoy international foods. And my greatest hope is that the recipes in this book will foster an understanding of how connected all cuisines are and how easily accessible the flavors are between food cultures.

(Note: In case you were wondering, I eat my fried bologna sandwich lightly toasted with Duke's mayonnaise and a fried egg, over medium. Don't forget to give your bologna a slit like a PAC-MAN face so you can caramelize the whole surface of the bologna in a skillet (it will curl up when it cooks if you don't). If there are any millennials reading this, just google PAC-MAN.

For example, my Cauliflower and Parsnip Soup (page 109) starts as a straightforward traditional European dish, but with the addition of cumin, it takes on a Southwestern flavor. Add chicken stock and a splash of white balsamic vinegar to lighten the cream and it takes on a delightful vegetable earthiness.

This crossover aspect of cuisines and ingredients became my particular area of interest and my guiding light in the kitchen early in my career. Sometimes, just to get folks fired up, I'd say something like, "Come by the house this weekend and have some chicken and gnocchi." My friends would say, "There you go again, cooking all that fancy stuff. Why don't you cook something that regular people eat." To which I would answer, "You mean something like chicken and dumplings? Because that's basically what this is."

I think it's important to have fun and be a little whimsical with food. I wish I could go back to when I was 10 years old so I could tell my grandmother that her fried pork chop was just pork schnitzel with a bone in it. Of course, now that I think about it, maybe that wouldn't go over so well with Granny.

To give you a bit of background on my road to Atlanta and my current restaurant, Southern National, let me start with my first food experiences. Mom and I lived in the projects outside Morgan City, where neighbors shared vegetables from their kitchen gardens. As early as I can remember, I cleaned fish and shrimp for my mom and put them in milk cartons that went into the deep freezer (this was before Tupperware, and the wax of the carton wouldn't disintegrate in the cold).

When we moved to Seattle, Mom was a nurse who often worked the 3 to 11 p.m. shift, so she taught me to cook for myself when I was just in elementary school. She showed me how to cook eggs in a Teflon pan so I didn't have to turn the heat too high, and I was so amazed, I ate a dozen eggs in one day. I didn't know there was anything wrong with that, I was just proud I could cook those eggs. I also learned to cook red beans and rice and those three items are still my favorite things to eat.

These days I use eggs more sparingly. My most popular egg dish at One Flew South at the Atlanta airport (more about this later) was the Dirty South, an open-faced meatloaf sandwich on pimento cheese with sautéed spinach and shallots, an over-easy egg on top, and Allan Benton's bacon with balsamic barbecue sauce.

By the time I was in high school, I cooked pretty well—and I also liked to play football. When I took a helmet to the knee in one game and was on crutches for a while, I was put into a Home Economics class. There were lots of girls and I liked to cook and make jokes, so I got along pretty well as the only male. The first thing the teacher taught us was how to make scones with homemade butter. I loved it! Here I was, a 6-foot 5-inch Black boy cooking with a bunch of giggling teenage girls and I was in heaven.

South Seattle Community College had a culinary program that was the best in the region and my high school teachers helped me get in. I was 14 years old when I toured the school and I knew that I wanted to do this for life.

Long work-story short, after college I worked my way up from cooking at a Safeway deli and a beachside café to apprenticing at an Italian restaurant and working at the Washington Athletic Club. By that time, I had read about the African American chefs who were making names for themselves: Patrick Clark (New York), Darryl Evans (Atlanta), and Johnny Rivers (Florida).

I called them all for work and Darryl was the only one who answered. I told him I wanted to cook the things I couldn't pronounce. He laughed, and I eventually ended up working for Evans at Occidental Grande—now the Four Seasons—from 1994 to 1997. From there, Darryl and I opened Spice Restaurant, serving modern American Southern food. It was wildly popular and drew a growing celebrity crowd of chefs, entertainers, and musicians. Usher was there for dinner one night and came to the kitchen to watch us cook. We regularly hosted celebs such as Michael Jordan, Monica Kaufman Pearson, Philippe Haddad (the chef at Abbey), Günter Seeger, and Daryl Shuler, the first African American master chef.

Growing up, I was always fascinated with humor and comedy. My dad was pretty silly in high school, so I must have inherited the laugh gene from him. At any rate, one of the ways I learned to relax early in my career was to head to a comedy club after my daytime chef job, take the stage for few minutes in my chef's hat, and entertain people with jokes about kitchen situations. I did improv at the Whole World Theater and Uptown Comedy Club in Atlanta, and in between, I did open mic nights 3 or 4 times a week, to learn how to write a joke. I started coming up with food jokes, and that's when I got funny and began to actually entertain the audience. I called myself the "Mad Chef." Most people with two jobs would say they wear two hats. In my case, I wear the same hat in the kitchen as I do on the comedy stage. What I've retained from this experience is the ability to find humor in negative situations and learn to laugh at myself. It's a great stress reliever.

My next job sort of combined both my talents. In 2000, I auditioned to be a spokesperson for the National Peanut Board. My last name is Nutter, so I thought I could do all right slinging peanuts. I was hired to entertain and cook, doing live demos at venues across the

FUN HAS ALWAYS BEEN A PART OF MY COOKING— IT SHOULDN'T BE STRESSFUL. I HOPE SOME OF THESE RECIPES AND STORIES WILL BRING A SMILE TO YOUR FACE.

country. We asked trivia questions and gave out aprons that said "I Cook for Peanuts" as prizes. It was sort of a traveling peanut museum sponsored by the peanut board in Georgia. On the road, we hit every state except Hawaii and Alaska. I wore a big hat shaped like a peanut (no, I will not show you a photo here), cooked a whole lot of peanut dishes, and told a lot of peanut jokes. Without a doubt, it gave me a lot of material for future comedy shows!

After that jaunt, Todd Richards offered me a job with him at a Ritz-Carlton in Florida and by 2004 we took it from the worst to the best hotel restaurant in the Ritz organization. In 2005, Todd and I were approached by Bobby Flay's producers for *Iron Chef America* to compete on a segment. We practiced for weeks without knowing what we'd cook until the show. We lost the competition by one point, but the judge thought we should have won. We actually got more press by losing and the publicity was great.

In 2008, two Black-owned companies were building a fine-dining restaurant with a sushi bar in the international wing at Hartsfield-Jackson Atlanta International Airport, and they were looking for chefs. With a new vision and challenge in mind, I accepted the position as One Flew South's executive chef and put my imagination to work on a menu that would blend Southern ingredients with world influences—an idea that fit for the first upscale travel/dining restaurant in the world's busiest airport. It became a big hit, even though you could only get reservations if you were flying in or out because it was on a concourse. Customers who wanted to be assured of a seat when they landed before or after an international flight could text or fax us their time and menu choices. We had regular customers who didn't even live in Georgia, and would text or call in their orders before they arrived at the airport or as their plane landed! It felt like a neighborhood restaurant, but the oddest one I'd ever seen.

Feeding travelers on the go at a busy airport is a very different experience than running a brick-and-mortar restaurant, and getting our menu right took some thought and a bit of luck. I noticed one day that a European flight landed daily near the restaurant around lunchtime and a number of French travelers arrived on it. Knowing that I've always loved French food, I came up with the idea of serving foie gras with a sweet potato purée and cherry vinegar sauce, which I figured would satisfy someone flying in from France who was hungry, tired, and not willing to eat a spicy burger or chicken tenders as their first meal in the States.

It was an immediate hit with the French travelers! The addition of this to our menu was a huge success, so I came up with more ideas, incorporating other influences—Japanese, Chinese, and South American, to name a few. I added mustard green chimichurri to a steak dish (Cast-Iron Seared New York Strip with Mojo Potatoes and Mustard Green Chimichurri on page 181). Many Europeans probably wouldn't try Southern mustard greens on their first taste of American cuisine but, surprisingly, the dish was a hit. In fact, like at One Flew South, I guarantee a surprise in every dish you try from this cookbook, such as the Mussels and Collard Greens with Toasted Baguette (page 139), in which collard green pot liquor is used to cook the mussels.

People who travel for work are a different type of customer and eater. One of those customers was "Wrong Answer Man" who became our best customer after a little incident. This man came in often and on one particular visit the airport plane train wasn't working, the security conveyor belt had ripped up his bag, and his flight was canceled. We didn't know this at first, and when he came into the restaurant all we saw was that he had only one shoe on and was holding the other—and he didn't look happy. He sat down, didn't look at the menu, and quickly ordered a scallop dish. The server told him that dish was no longer on the menu and his immediate and forceful response was, "WRONG ANSWER!" Our manager went to his table to see what the problem was and the man explained all the ways his day had gone wrong and how he had thought his day would be all right if only he could have the scallop dish he had enjoyed on a previous trip. He left happy, but "wrong answer" became a back-of-the-house joke.

For several years now, I've worked on expanding the definition of contemporary Southern food. I like to say that I'm a Southern chef who eats more fried chicken than I cook—much like Edward Lee who once said he was the Asian guy that didn't do sushi. It's not that I strive to create a type of fusion; it's that I have learned to take the best of regional and international cuisines and use them to make Southern food even better—and eventually reach a larger audience.

Using authentic, fresh, seasonal ingredients is the core of good cooking and a major part of this book. With any recipe I create, I ask myself: If I can't get fresh basil, what else would an Italian grandmother use in season to create a great pesto? And don't worry, these recipes don't call for tons of spices you'll never use again. Basically a thrifty person, I never buy an ingredient that I can't use in several dishes.

Southern National is the name of the restaurant I first opened in Mobile, Alabama, that is now located in Atlanta, Georgia. The name is also a perfect description of where I've been, where I'm at, and where I'm headed with food—much like the many people I've served over the years and the food I've cooked for them. I promise there is nothing in this book that will be alien to you if you love Southern food. For traditionalists, these recipes are firmly rooted in Southern sensibilities, but with a little something new. Something tasty. Something fun.

Fun has always been a part of my cooking. Cooking shouldn't be stressful. I hope some of these recipes and stories will bring a smile to your face. (Like any good performer, a chef knows they can't please everyone.) Over the years, these recipes have been judged by critical diners in my restaurants and have been chosen and written with an eye to the ease and simplicity that home cooks demand. To that end, seasoned cooks as well as beginners will enjoy the opportunity to make comfort foods with a new blast of flavors or a twist in the preparation.

I hope you have as much fun in your kitchen cooking these recipes as I've had creating them for you. Let the show begin!

THE SETUP

≡ FAVORITE COCKTAILS AND IMPROVISED CLASSICS ≡

APEROL SPRITZ

I was late coming to the Aperol spritz party—didn't have my first one until I was a guest chef with my buddy Todd Richards on a Holland America Cruise. We were on the boat for two weeks and cooked for four days. We walked around Monaco the day after Louis Hamilton won the Grand Prix there. Best of all, we got to drive the F1 course in a Ferrari—it was a humbling experience. Some poor guy broke up with his girlfriend and was giving rides to tourists to raise money to get back home. Every time I have one of these drinks, I wonder if he made it home. SERVES 1

3 ounces Aperol

3 ounces dry prosecco

1 ounce unflavored club soda
   or sparkling water

Orange slice, for garnish

Fill a big wineglass with ice until it is nearly full. Pour in the Aperol (I usually eyeball this and pour until I've filled about one-third of the glass).

Pour in an equal amount of prosecco. Top off your drink with a splash of club soda and add a slice of orange.

BAR GARNISHES

Coin: A silver-dollar-size circle cut from the peel of the surface of the fruit, folded in half, and pinched to express the peel into the drink, then floated in the glass.

Swath: A swath is a thicker piece of the citrus rind that has more oil than a twist. It is rubbed around the rim of the glass so you get the taste when you sip, then often discarded.

Twist: A slice of citrus zest used for decoration and to add flavor to the mixed drink.

Wedge: A triangular slice of fruit, often with a notch cut into it to sit on the rim of the glass. The shape of a wedge allows the drinker to squeeze some juice into the drink for added flavor.

Wheel or Slice: A ¼-inch-thick round slice of fruit, with a slit cut halfway through to sit on the rim of the glass.

ARMAGNAC OLD-FASHIONED

I think of this drink as the next level for old-fashioned fans, and for those who like their spirits straight. The 15-year-old Armagnac adds the youth you may be looking for! SERVES 1

2 dashes Regan's Orange Bitters

1 dash Angostura bitters

1 bar spoon sorghum syrup

1 ounce soda water

1¾ ounces Chateau de Briat 15-year-old Armagnac

1 orange coin (peel, no pith)

Build this drink in a rocks glass. Combine all the ingredients except the garnish, and give it a long stir. Top with 1 or 2 ice cubes as needed, and garnish with the lemon swath.

Note: A bar spoon is equal to a standard teaspoon.

BOURBON OLD-FASHIONED

My good friends Walter Leffler and Jerry Slater hooked me on these drinks while we were sipping with bourbon legends, Julian van Winkle III and Chris Morris. SERVES 1

1 teaspoon powdered sugar or 1 sugar cube

3 dashes Angostura bitters

1 teaspoon water

2 ounces bourbon or rye, whiskey dealer's choice

1 orange twist and 1 lemon swath, for garnish (it's not traditional but neither am I!)

Combine the sugar and bitters to a mixing glass. Add the water and stir until the sugar is nearly dissolved.

Fill the mixing glass with ice, add the bourbon, and stir until well chilled. Strain into a rocks glass filled with one large ice cube.

Express the oil of the orange twist and lemon swath over the glass, and then drop them into the glass to garnish.

BLACKBERRY-TEQUILA SMASH

I notice that tequila usually gets people fired up. It could be that's where the term "liquid courage" comes from. If you are not really the type to smash up the bar, this is the tequila drink for you. Let's just call this one a smash hit. SERVES 1

6 fresh blackberries

6 small mint leaves

2 ounces añejo tequila

½ ounce agave syrup

½ ounce fresh lime juice

2 ounces club soda or Sprite

In a cocktail shaker, combine the fresh blackberries and mint leaves and muddle with a spoon until the berries are completely macerated.

Add the tequila, agave syrup, lime juice, and about ½ cup ice. Cover, and give it a good shake for 20 to 30 seconds.

Double strain the drink into a glass filled with crushed ice. Top off the drink with the soda water or Sprite. Give it a stir and garnish with the muddled blackberries and mint.

BOULEVARDIER

Loosely translated, a boulevardier is a man-about-town; please note, however, that this is *not* a gender-based cocktail. It's for everyone. SERVES 1

1¼ ounces bourbon or rye

1 ounce Campari

1 ounce sweet vermouth

Orange twist, for garnish

Fill a large mixing glass with ice. Pour in the bourbon, Campari, and sweet vermouth. Stir until well chilled.

Strain into a rocks glass over fresh ice. (Sometime I like it neat, too.) Garnish with the orange twist.

SPICED-RUM ICED COFFEE

This is a good alternative to a Bailey's and Cream. I added it to my menu when I opened a restaurant in Mobile, Alabama. The rum connection between Cuba, the Virgin Islands, and Mobile goes back hundreds of years, so we always kept a good selection of rum for the locals. SERVES 1

2 ounces spiced rum

5 ounces cold brew coffee

1 ounce sweetened condensed milk

Combine all the ingredients in a cocktail shaker. Cover, and shake well. Pour into a glass over ice, or serve it in a coffee cup and pretend it is still prohibition!

RASPBERRY-BASIL PUNCH

I came up with this idea when I was hired to do a dinner in the Hamptons. The host had the wine for the dinner, but hadn't planned a drink for the cocktail service. I had some vodka and extra raspberries with me, and this drink was such a success I still serve it. SERVES 1

1 ounce Raspberry Syrup (see below)

1½ ounces honeysuckle vodka, or your favorite vodka

1½ ounces sparkling wine, club soda, or lemon-lime soda

Fill a cocktail shaker half to three-quarters full with ice.

Pour in the Raspberry Syrup. Add the honeysuckle vodka, cover, and shake for about 10 seconds, or until the shaker begins to frost and is cool to the touch. Stir the soda or sparkling wine of your choice into the shaker.

Strain the cocktail into a chilled cocktail glass.

Note: If you want more basil flavor, muddle a few leaves in your cocktail glass, then fill with ice. To mocktail it, bypass the vodka and wine, double the amount of club soda or lemon-lime soda, and substitute lemon juice for the lime juice.

RASPBERRY SYRUP

MAKES 1½ TO 2 CUPS

1 pint raspberries, rinsed

1 cup agave syrup or honey (add more or less depending on the sweetness of the raspberries)

8 basil leaves

2 ounces fresh lime juice

1 star anise pod

Combine the raspberries, agave syrup, basil, lime juice, and star anise in a blender, and blend until smooth. Strain the syrup through a fine-mesh sieve into a bowl to remove the seeds and star anise pod. Transfer to a lidded jar and refrigerate for up to 3 weeks.

ON THE NOSE

This bourbon, lime, ginger, soda, and dark rum float leads the parade! It is a good alternative for those who like a Dark-N-Stormy, Whiskey Sour, or Whiskey-Ginger. SERVES 1

2 dashes Angostura bitters

¼ ounce cane syrup

½ ounce ginger syrup

¾ ounce fresh lime juice

1½ ounces Nelson Bros. Classic Bourbon

1½ ounces soda water

1 teaspoon of Worthy Park 109 Dark Rum

1 lime wedge, for garnish

Build this drink in a cocktail shaker partially filled with ice, combining the bitters, cane syrup, ginger syrup, lime juice, and bourbon. Cover and shake.

Fill a collins glass with ice and strain the drink into it. Top with the soda water and stir to combine.

Using a bar spoon, float the rum on top and garnish with a lime wedge.

Note: Any drink that has citrus in it needs to be shaken to aerate the cocktail as well as to balance and dilute the acidity.

COCONUT NEGRONI

Coconut gin is rare, but you can find it online and it's worth having if you like flavored gins. You smell the coconut more than taste it, so it doesn't bring that sweet heaviness that coconut usually does—this is a light drink. If you can't enjoy this while vacationing on the Mediterranean, you can still enjoy the sensory experience with this drink.

Good for Negroni drinkers and lovers of slightly off-center, bitter drinks. SERVES 1

1¼ ounces Bimini Coconut Gin

1¼ ounces Carpano Classico
  Red Vermouth

1¼ ounces Campari

Orange twist, for garnish

Build this drink in a mixing glass filled with 4 to 5 ice cubes, combining the gin, vermouth, and Campari. Stir until well chilled, then strain into a rocks glass, straight up or over ice. You can also mix the drink directly in a rocks glass.

Rub the rim with the orange twist and drop it in the drink as garnish.

SAZERAC COCKTAIL

A Creole apothecarist named Antoine Peychaud invented the Sazerac at his French Quarter pharmacy on Royal Street in New Orleans in the 1800s. Why do I like Sazerac rye so much? It's a mild whiskey, so you can taste the other flavors of the drink. It stands up, but doesn't overpower—like me! I'm six foot five, but I'm really gentle. SERVES 1

1 sugar cube

3 dashes Peychaud's Bitters

2 ounces Sazerac rye whiskey

¼ ounce absinthe, or anise liqueur

Lemon twist, for garnish

First, fill an old-fashioned glass with ice cubes and let chill. Then use a yarai (mixing) glass to mix the cocktail.

Soak the sugar cube with the bitters in the mixing glass, and muddle with a spoon to crush the cube and make a paste. Add the rye and some ice cubes, and stir to properly dilute and chill.

Discard the ice in the old-fashioned glass, then coat the glass with the absinthe, discarding any extra liquor.

Pour the whiskey into the absinthe-coated glass, garnish with the lemon twist, and serve.

THE SOUTHERN NATIONAL

We invented this drink to feature the whiskey and bourbon from African American distillers. Nathan Nearest (Uncle Nearest), a freed slave, was the man who trained Mr. Jack to make Jack Daniel's about 150 years ago. Nearest instituted a charcoal distilling method from West Africa, and the result is a legendary liquor. The Uncle Nearest bourbon brand is currently produced in Kentucky by one of his descendants, master blender Victoria Eady Butler. SERVES 1

1 dash Angostura bitters

1 dash Peychaud's bitters

¼ ounce Cocchi Americano

¾ ounce Carpano Classico vermouth

1 ounce Uncle Nearest bourbon

1 ounce Rye and Sons rye whiskey

1 lemon swath

Build the drink in a mixing glass over ice, combining the Angostura and Peychaud's bitters, Cocchi Americano, vermouth, bourbon, and whiskey. Stir, then strain into a rocks glass over 4 or 5 ice cubes. Garnish with the lemon swath.

RUM SWEET TEA (OFF-DAY PORCH PUNCH)

This is an after work, hot day, people-watching drink. You could dress it up or down in a collins glass or dumped into a pitcher like sweet tea. Just remember to use lots of ice. SERVES 6 TO 8

3 cups water

½ cup cane sugar

3 black tea bags

1 lemon, sliced into wedges

1 orange, sliced into wedges

1 lime, sliced into wedges

1 cup rum of choice

Lime wheels, for garnish

4 sprigs mint

In a small saucepan, combine the water and sugar and bring to a boil over high heat. Turn down the heat to maintain a simmer and cook, stirring, until all the sugar is dissolved.

Pour the sugar water into a jar or pitcher and add the tea bags. Let steep for 10 to 15 minutes. If you want it less strong, let it steep for 5 to 10 minutes.

Remove and discard the tea bags. Add the lemon, orange, and lime wedges and rum and mix well. Refrigerate until chilled. To enjoy, pour into glasses with lots of ice, and garnish with the lime wheels and mint.

STOCK MATERIAL

= SAUCES AND CONDIMENTS =

BASIC SONAT RUB

A basic dry rub is a mixture of spices and/or herbs that is applied to food for the purpose of adding flavor. I feel like rubs are a pantry essential. They can be as simple or as complex as you like, which I find really interesting.

This all-purpose workhorse rub can be used on big pieces of meat such as pork butt or brisket. In smaller amounts it can be used on fish and shrimp. MAKES A LITTLE OVER 1 CUP

2 tablespoons kosher salt

¼ cup paprika

2 tablespoons sugar

2 tablespoons granulated garlic

2 tablespoons granulated onion

2 tablespoons dark chili powder

1 teaspoon cayenne pepper

1 tablespoon curry powder

1 tablespoon ground cumin

1 tablespoon freshly ground
   black pepper

2 teaspoons ground ginger

In a small bowl, stir all the ingredients together. Use immediately, or store in an airtight container at room temperature for up 3 months.

COFFEE RUB

Don't make the mistake of thinking this will make your meat taste like coffee. A coffee rub adds an earthy undertone and balances the sweetness of the sugar—rounding the flavor out. Sugar helps you get a crust on the meat and coffee pushes the sweetness to the back burner, so you don't taste the sugar first. MAKES ABOUT 1 CUP

3 tablespoons finely ground coffee

2 tablespoons brown sugar

1 tablespoon kosher salt

1 tablespoon smoked paprika

2 teaspoons granulated onion

2 teaspoons granulated garlic

1 teaspoon cumin

½ teaspoon cayenne pepper

2 teaspoons mustard powder

1 tablespoon ground coriander

In a small bowl, use a fork or a small whisk to mix together all the ingredients until well combined. Use immediately, or store in an airtight container at room temperature for up 2 months.

SONAT EVERYTHING SEASONING

As far as spice seasoning blends goes, this one takes best of show. It's the addition of the red pepper flakes that gives it a little heat. I like to sprinkle it on a salad, on buttered toast, or on my bagels with cream cheese. MAKES ABOUT 3 CUPS

½ cup dried minced onion

½ cup dried minced garlic

¼ cup poppy seeds

½ cup black sesame seeds

½ cup white sesame seeds

¼ cup fennel seeds

3 tablespoons red pepper flakes

3 tablespoons smoked flaky salt

In a medium bowl, stir all the ingredients together and mix well. Store in an airtight container in a cool, dry place for up to 2 months.

CANE SYRUP BUTTER

Steens Cane Syrup was one of the many things my family would get shipped to Seattle from our home state of Louisiana before there was Amazon. I would call my uncle in Louisiana and he would pack it in some dry ice and ship it to me on the bus—a great care package! MAKES 2 CUPS

1 pound (4 sticks) unsalted butter, at room temperature

¾ cup cane syrup

1 teaspoon smoked salt

Whisk all the ingredients together in a large bowl until combined. Use it immediately or cover and refrigerate for up to 2 weeks.

MUSTARD GREEN BUTTER

If you're a fan of mustard greens (and who isn't?), this compound butter is a delicious addition when cooking oysters, steaks, grilled swordfish, shrimp, and pasta. MAKES 2 CUPS

1 tablespoon kosher salt, for blanching

4 mustard green leaves, stems removed

1 pound (4 sticks) unsalted butter

½ bunch flat-leaf parsley

Zest of 1 lemon

1 teaspoon alderwood smoked
    salt or smoked salt of choice

Prepare an ice bath in a large bowl with ice and water, for blanching.

In a medium saucepan, combine 4 cups water and the salt and bring to a boil over medium-high heat. Add the mustard greens and blanch for 2 minutes. Transfer the greens to the ice bath to cool for 5 to 10 minutes. Drain the mustard green leaves and pat dry with paper towels. Place the greens in a food processor and process until smooth.

Add the butter, parsley, lemon zest, and smoked salt and blitz until smooth. Wrap in plastic wrap and refrigerate for up to 2 weeks in the refrigerator or up to 3 months in the freezer.

SAGE COMPOUND BUTTER

This is my go-to compound butter for grilled steaks or pork chops. At room temperature, it's what I apply to the meat after cooking, while it rests. It also works well with any pasta—just add the drained pasta to a pan on the stove with a little pasta water and a pat of this butter—stir and serve. For purists like me, you can't beat it simply served on toast or slathered on a biscuit.

MAKES 2 CUPS

1 head garlic (about 15 cloves)

1 tablespoon extra-virgin olive oil

Kosher salt

Freshly ground black pepper

1 pound (4 sticks) butter, at room temperature

1 tablespoon Worcestershire sauce

2 tablespoons chopped sage

Preheat the oven to 400 degrees F.

Peel the papery skin from the outside of the garlic head. Cut ¼ inch off the top of the head of garlic to expose the cloves. Discard the top portion. Place the garlic on a sheet of aluminum foil and drizzle with olive oil. Sprinkle with salt and pepper, wrap the garlic completely in the foil, and roast 40 to 50 minutes, until the cloves are soft and tender. Set aside to cool, then use a cocktail fork or your fingers to squeeze the garlic out of the roasted cloves.

In a stand mixer, combine the butter, roasted garlic, Worcestershire sauce, and sage, and mix until smooth.

You can either transfer the butter to an airtight container or a glass jar, or roll the butter into a log and wrap it up with parchment or wax paper. Store for up to 2 weeks in the refrigerator or up to 3 months if you freeze.

SMOKED PAPRIKA COMPOUND BUTTER

I like to use this on Grilled Lobster Tail, circa 1995 (page 133), and pretty much any seafood—grilled shrimp, swordfish, and sautéed clams—as well as steaks. MAKES ABOUT 1 CUP

½ pound (2 sticks) unsalted butter, at room temperature

2 tablespoons capers, drained and chopped.

3 tablespoons chopped flat-leaf parsley

2 tablespoons chopped shallots

2 tablespoons Worcestershire sauce

½ teaspoon smoked paprika

½ teaspoon paprika

¼ teaspoon red pepper flakes

In a food processor, combine all the ingredients and blitz until smooth, scraping the sides of the bowl as needed. Scoop the butter onto a 10-inch-long piece of plastic wrap or parchment paper and roll into a log. Chill for at least 1 hour before serving.

Refrigerate, wrapped in plastic wrap, for up to 2 weeks in the refrigerator and up to 3 months in the freezer.

ROASTED GARLIC-HERB BUTTER

Parsley and thyme pairs well with just about any savory dish, but fresh herbs can be used with this recipe. You can be naughty or nice with this treat—use it as much or as little as you like on your favorite dishes. Add a dollop to your steak when it's finished cooking, or baste a seared piece of fish with it. Anything you like to put butter on, sage butter is good on.

MAKES A LITTLE MORE THAN 1 POUND

2 heads garlic

1 tablespoon extra-virgin olive oil

1 pound (4 sticks) unsalted butter, at room temperature

3 tablespoons chopped fresh herbs (parsley, thyme, rosemary, and/or chives)

Preheat the oven to 400 degrees F.

Peel the papery skin from the outside of the garlic head. Cut ¼ inch off the top of the head of garlic to expose the cloves. Discard the top portion.

Place the garlic on a sheet of aluminum foil and drizzle with the olive oil. Wrap the garlic completely in the foil, and roast for 40 to 50 minutes, or until the garlic is soft throughout and lightly browned. (I use lightly browned garlic for finishing butters; and garlic cooked to just soft for cooking meat at high temperature, or for basting.) Set aside to cool, then use a cocktail fork or your fingers to squeeze the garlic out of the roasted cloves.

In a food processor, combine the butter, herbs, and roasted garlic and blitz until smooth.

You can either transfer the butter to an airtight container or a glass jar, or roll the butter into a log and wrap it up with parchment or wax paper. Store for up to 2 weeks in the refrigerator or up to 3 months in the freezer.

GARLIC OIL

I use this in place of plain olive oil for grilling vegetables, roasting potatoes, and toasting baguettes. I also put it on the tater tots at the restaurant! It's a time-saver and a treat if you love garlic.

MAKES 2 CUPS

1 head garlic

2 cups extra-virgin olive oil

To prepare garlic, remove the skin, lay a clove flat on a cutting board, put the flat of a knife on top, and smash down with your hand to spread the fibers. Repeat for all the cloves.

Transfer the garlic to a medium saucepan, add the olive oil, and heat over medium-low for 3 to 4 minutes until bubbles form around the garlic, then give it a stir.

Continue to cook for 10 to 15 minutes, or until the garlic is golden brown. Set aside the pan to cool to room temperature. Think of this like making tea; you're not just mixing two ingredients; you're steeping the garlic in the oil.

Strain the oil through a fine-mesh sieve to remove the smashed garlic. (You can save the garlic to spread on toast or add to your favorite mashed potatoes recipe.)

Store the oil in an airtight container in the refrigerator for up to 1 week.

ROASTED GARLIC AIOLI

This makes the perfect amount for an immersion blender, but I prefer using a food processor because you get a more consistent product, that adds volume to the finish—not to mention the convenience of speed. MAKES 2 ½ TO 3 CUPS

1 head garlic

1 teaspoon kosher salt plus more as needed

Freshly ground black pepper

2 cups extra-virgin olive oil or canola oil, divided

2 eggs

2 egg yolks

2 tablespoons Dijon mustard

2 tablespoons lemon juice

2 teaspoons Worcestershire sauce

1 tablespoon Tabasco or SoNat Fermented Hot Sauce (page 66)

Preheat the oven to 400 degrees F.

Peel the papery skin from the outside of the garlic head. Cut ¼ inch off the top of the head of garlic to expose the cloves. Discard the top portion.

Place the garlic on a sheet of aluminum foil, generously season with salt and pepper, and drizzle with 2 tablespoons olive oil. Wrap the garlic completely in the foil, and roast for 40 to 50 minutes, or until the garlic is soft throughout and lightly browned. Set aside to cool, then use a cocktail fork or your fingers to squeeze the garlic out of the roasted cloves. Place the roasted garlic into the bowl of a food processor.

Place the eggs, egg yolks, mustard, lemon juice, 1 teaspoon salt, Worcestershire sauce, and Tabasco in the food processor with the garlic. Pulse a couple of times to combine and, with the food processor on, slowly add half the remaining oil and process until the emulsification process begins to take place. Turn off the food processor and scrape down the sides of the bowl. Continue adding oil and processing until the aioli thickens. If you want a lighter texture, simply add more oil.

Store the aioli in an airtight container in the refrigerator for up to 2 weeks.

BUTTERMILK DRESSING

The best part of this homemade dressing is that you taste all the herbs, as well as the zippiness of the fresh buttermilk. You just can't get this from a shelf-stable dressing. If you have leftover roasted beets, this is a perfect way to use them. The beets add sweetness to this recipe.

MAKES ABOUT 3 CUPS

1 cup buttermilk

1/2 cup sour cream

1/2 cup diced roasted golden beets

1 teaspoon garlic powder

3/4 cup Duke's mayonnaise

2 teaspoons finely chopped tarragon

1 teaspoon dried chives

Zest and juice of 1/2 lemon

2 teaspoons Tabasco hot sauce

2 tablespoons Worcestershire sauce

2 teaspoons kosher salt

1 teaspoon freshly ground black pepper

To make the buttermilk dressing, place the buttermilk, sour cream, beets, and garlic powder in a blender, and blend until well combined and the beets are creamy.

Pour the mixture into a large bowl. Add the mayonnaise, tarragon, chives, lemon zest and juice, Tabasco, Worcestershire sauce, salt, and pepper and whisk together until well combined.

The dressing can be refrigerated in an airtight container for up to 1 week.

CURRY-MUSTARD SPREAD

Good with duck or pulled pork. Makes for a delicious duck sandwich. MAKES A LITTLE MORE THAN 2 CUPS

2 cups Duke's mayonnaise

1 tablespoon whole-grain mustard

2 teaspoons curry powder

1 teaspoon ground cumin

1 teaspoon freshly ground black pepper

Zest and juice of 1 lemon

Combine all the ingredients in a large bowl and mix well. Transfer to an airtight container, refrigerate, and store for up to 3 weeks. But I'm sure you will finish it before then.

MUSTARD GREEN CHIMICHURRI

The first time I tasted this classic Argentinian sauce, I was about 21 years young and attending an event on the rooftop space at the Occidental Grand Hotel, now the Atlanta Four Seasons. I have since given it a Southern touch with the addition of mustard greens, and it has become one of my favorite sauces to cook with. If you want a less consistent, chunkier sauce, use a food processor, but I like to make this with a blender so it's smoother. This may be one of the most versatile sauces on earth. It tastes good on grilled meats, braised meat, roasted veggies, and grilled veggies. I also use this as a steak sauce, on oysters, as a dip for sandwiches, and on woodfire-grilled lobster tails. You can add a little more oil and use it as a salad dressing too. Just have fun with it! MAKES 1½ CUPS

2 cups flat-leaf parsley

3 cups stems removed and greens coarsely chopped mustard greens (save the stems for the Pickled Okra and Collard Green Stems on page 76)

1 cup fresh cilantro

10 garlic cloves

6 tablespoons red wine vinegar

2 teaspoons dried oregano or 2 tablespoons fresh oregano

2 teaspoons red pepper flakes

1 teaspoon kosher salt

1 teaspoon freshly ground black pepper

2 cups extra-virgin olive oil

Combine the parsley, mustard greens, cilantro, garlic, vinegar, oregano, red pepper flakes, salt, and pepper in a blender. With the blender running, drizzle in the olive oil. Blend 3 to 5 minutes, until it is a consistent, dark green purée.

Store in an airtight container in the refrigerator for up to 2 weeks, or you can freeze it for up to 2 months.

JAZZED-UP HOISIN SAUCE

This is a thick, sweet condiment that makes a tasty dip, marinade, glaze, or stir-fry sauce.
MAKES 1½ CUPS

1 cup hoisin sauce

1 tablespoon sesame oil

1 teaspoon ground coriander

1 (½-inch) knob ginger, peeled
   and shaved on a Microplane

⅛ teaspoon freshly ground
   black pepper

In a small bowl, whisk together the hoisin sauce, ½ cup water, sesame oil, coriander, ginger, and pepper. Refrigerate in an airtight container for up to 2 weeks.

COMEBACK SAUCE

Here's a sauce that goes well with oysters, poached shrimp, and the Corn and Andouille Fritters (page 91). Basically this is a spicy rémoulade sauce for those who want an extra kick out of their seafood. MAKES ABOUT ¾ CUP

½ cup Duke's mayonnaise

2 tablespoons ketchup

2 tablespoons SoNat Fermented Hot
   Sauce (page 66) or store-bought

2 teaspoons Worcestershire sauce

½ teaspoon garlic powder

½ teaspoon onion powder

¼ teaspoon freshly ground
   black pepper

Mix all the ingredients together in a small bowl until smooth. Transfer to an airtight container and refrigerate for up to 1 month.

PECAN-BASIL PESTO

If an Italian grandmother lived in the American South and there were no pine nuts available, I'm sure she would substitute pecans. I tried it and liked it! Everyone hears pesto and thinks "basil," but actually pesto is the cooking technique of using a mortar and pestle. You can make pesto a day ahead. Just top with some oil to prevent browning. MAKES ABOUT 2 CUPS

½ cup pecan pieces

2 cups packed fresh basil leaves

1 cup shredded Parmesan cheese

3 garlic cloves

¼ cup lemon juice

½ cup extra-virgin olive oil

½ teaspoon kosher salt

½ teaspoon freshly ground
    black pepper

Zest of 2 small lemons

Preheat the oven to 350 degrees F.

Spread out the pecans on a baking sheet and toast in the over for 8 to 10 minutes, giving them a toss about halfway through the cooking time, until they are evenly browned.

Let the pecans cool, then combine them in a food processor with the basil, cheese, garlic, lemon juice, and olive oil. Process until smooth, then add the salt, pepper, and lemon zest and pulse until combined.

Refrigerate in an airtight container for up to 3 weeks, or freeze for up to 2 months.

BALSAMIC BARBECUE SAUCE

I like to use this on a meatloaf sandwich (it's also baked into the Asian Meatloaf, page 176), and the Barbecue Pork Pizza (page 171). You don't need an aged or fortified flavored vinegar. A basic balsamic lets the smoky taste shine. MAKES ABOUT 2 ½ QUARTS

2 cups balsamic vinegar

3 cups ketchup

1½ cups molasses

1 cup whole-grain mustard

¾ cup Worcestershire sauce

1 cup light brown sugar

2 tablespoons dry mustard

2 tablespoons onion powder

2 tablespoons garlic powder

1 bouquet garni (½ bunch fresh thyme and 1 bay leaf, tied with butcher's twine)

In a large saucepan over medium-low heat, combine all the ingredients, mixing well to incorporate. Simmer for 30 minutes.

The sauce will be thick in consistency, so add water to thin it to your liking. Remove the bouquet garni before serving.

Refrigerate in an airtight container for up to 3 weeks.

SONAT MOJO SAUCE

You gotta have mojo to really like this sauce—it's bold, spicy, and not for the fainthearted. You'll love it. MAKES ABOUT 3 CUPS

2 red bell peppers, roasted, peeled, cored, and seeded

2 whole habañero peppers, stemmed

½ cup orange juice

5 garlic cloves

3 tablespoons sherry vinegar

1 tablespoon ground cumin

1 tablespoon coriander seeds

2 green onions, trimmed

2 tablespoons Worcestershire sauce

½ cup extra-virgin olive oil

1 teaspoon kosher salt

Place all the ingredients in a blender and blitz until smooth. Adjust the seasoning to your liking. Refrigerate in an airtight container for up to 1 week.

CHERRY-MISO SAUCE

I developed this sauce back when I was the chef at the Oak Room in Louisville Kentucky. It has followed me to all the other places I have worked. It goes great with fish and with game meats. So far, my favorite way to enjoy the sauce is on the Seared Redfish with Field Peas, Green Beans, Smoked Turkey, and Cherry-Miso Sauce (page 142). MAKES 2 CUPS

2 tablespoons fresh ginger, peeled, and chopped

1 large shallot, coarsely chopped

¼ cup white balsamic vinegar

¼ cup sugar

2 cups dried cherries

1½ cups orange juice

2½ tablespoons miso paste

2 teaspoons dried thyme

1 teaspoon ground ginger

Combine all the ingredients in a saucepan over medium heat and cook for 20 minutes. Transfer to a blender and purée until smooth. It will have the thick consistency of honey.

Refrigerate in an airtight container for up to 4 weeks.

WHISKEY TARTAR SAUCE

I made this sauce for my Uncle Bob, a man of few words, at a family fish fry. His comment was, "You can stay in the family, Shinery (my middle name). You're all right." MAKES ABOUT 4 CUPS

2 cups Duke's mayonnaise

1 cup chopped bread-and-butter pickles

2 tablespoons chopped fresh parsley

3 tablespoons chopped green onion

Zest and juice of 1 lemon

2 teaspoons whole-grain Dijon mustard

1 teaspoon granulated garlic

1 teaspoon Worcestershire sauce

½ teaspoon Tabasco sauce

2 ounces whiskey

½ teaspoon kosher salt

½ teaspoon freshly ground black pepper

Combine all the ingredients in a large bowl and whisk until well incorporated. Adjust the seasoning by adding more salt and pepper if needed. Refrigerate until ready to use.

Refrigerate in an airtight container for up to 3 weeks.

CURRY YOGURT SAUCE

This is a great addition to roasted lamb, potatoes, or in the Loaded Sweet Potato recipe (page 156).

MAKES 2 ½ CUPS

2 cups plain Greek yogurt

1 tablespoon curry powder

1 teaspoon ground cumin

1 teaspoon dried dill

1 jalapeño, seeded and diced

Juice and zest of 1 lime

¼ teaspoon kosher salt

¼ teaspoon freshly ground
   black pepper

In a medium bowl, combine all the ingredients and whisk together until incorporated. Adjust the seasoning if needed.

Refrigerate in an airtight container for up to 2 weeks.

PIZZA SAUCE

This is a good basic tomato sauce to have on hand for pizza night. MAKES ENOUGH SAUCE FOR 6 (10-INCH) PIZZAS

3 cups or 1 (28-ounce) can whole
San Marzano tomatoes

1 teaspoon oregano

½ teaspoon granulated garlic

½ teaspoon granulated onion

1 teaspoon red pepper flakes

1 teaspoon kosher salt

½ teaspoon freshly ground
black pepper

1 tablespoon extra-virgin olive oil

Combine all the ingredients in a food processor and blend until smooth.

Refrigerate in an airtight container for up to 1 week.

SONAT RED-EYE GRAVY

This is my version of the classic red-eye gravy. For starters, what makes mine so different is the number of ingredients. For the classic version, all you need is some country ham and strong coffee. This version is rich and savory. The veal stock cuts the bitterness of the coffee. This recipe can be halved. MAKES 2 ½ QUARTS

Extra-virgin olive oil

3 slices Benton's bacon, cut into ½-inch lardons

4 garlic cloves, smashed

½ cup medium-dice onion (about half an onion)

2 bay leaves

½ cup coffee beans

2 cups D's Chicken Stock (page 71) or store-bought

3 quarts veal stock

¼ bunch thyme

Kosher salt

Freshly ground black pepper

Heat a little oil in a large stockpot or Dutch oven over medium heat. Add the bacon and cook, stirring, to render the fat. When the bacon is almost cooked, add the garlic, onion, and bay leaves and cook 3 to 5 minutes, or until the veggies and bacon are golden brown.

Add the coffee beans, chicken stock, veal stock, and thyme, stir, and simmer for 15 minutes, until the flavors come together and the gravy thickens. If the gravy is too thick, add a little more chicken stock. Add salt and pepper to taste. Strain the gravy and discard the solids before you serve.

Refrigerate in an airtight container for up to 7 days.

SONAT FERMENTED HOT SAUCE

No more buying hot sauce with this easy homemade version. MAKES A LITTLE MORE THAN 4 CUPS

1 teaspoon coriander seeds, toasted

1½ pounds Fresno peppers, or peppers of choice, tops and stems removed, and halved

6 garlic cloves

1 ounce fresh ginger, peeled and coarsely chopped

4 cups filtered or spring water

4 teaspoons kosher salt

⅓ cup rice wine vinegar

1 tablespoon cane syrup or maple syrup

½ teaspoon xanthan gum (a thickener), optional

Toast the coriander seeds in a small dry skillet over medium-high heat for 1½ minutes until the seeds become fragrant.

Divide the peppers, garlic, coriander seeds, and ginger between 2 clean, wide-mouth 1-quart canning jars.

To make a brine, heat the water and the salt in a medium saucepan until the salt has dissolved completely. Set aside to cool to room temperature.

Pour the brine over the pepper mixtures, completely submerging them.

Fit the jars with a fermentation lid or cheesecloth secured with a rubber band. Place them in a warm, dark place for 5 to 7 days, or until the brine looks cloudy and small bubbles begin to appear when you tap the side of the jar. Make sure the peppers stay submerged under the brine during the entire fermentation process to prevent mold growth.

When the fermentation time is up, strain the brine into a bowl. Place the fermented pepper mixture in a blender, add 1 cup of the brine, the rice wine vinegar, and cane syrup. Blend until completely smooth. You can add additional brine to reach the desired thickness.

While the blender is running, sprinkle in the xanthan gum, if using, and blend for an additional 1 minute. Strain into a bowl through a fine-mesh strainer lined with cheesecloth and remove all the pulp. (You can dry the pulp and use it as a spicy seasoning!)

Transfer the hot sauce to bottles or sealed containers, and refrigerate for up to 6 months. If you haven't used the xanthan gum, the sauce will separate after storage. Just shake it up every time you use it.

Notes: If you are using cheesecloth during fermentation, you will need to use some kind of weight to keep your pepper mixture completely submerged. I like to use a ziplock sandwich bag filled with water to help submerge the ingredients. If you own a fermenting container, then just follow the manufacturer's instructions. When you handle peppers, wear gloves and wash your hands extremely well.

PEPPER JELLY

This tasty jam has become a staple in our kitchen and I started making it just so my peppers wouldn't go bad! MAKES 2 (12-OUNCE) JARS

1 red bell pepper, stemmed, seeded, and diced

1 yellow bell pepper, stemmed, seeded, and diced

1 pound jalapeño peppers, stemmed, and seeds removed from half of them

5 cups sugar

1¼ cups apple cider vinegar

1 teaspoon kosher salt

2 teaspoons ground ginger

1 (1.75-ounce) package Sure-Jell pectin (available at the grocery store)

¼ cup lemon juice

Use a food processor to blitz the bell peppers and jalapeños until they are finely chopped. Transfer the peppers to paper towels or cheesecloth and squeeze out any excess liquid.

Combine the chopped peppers, sugar, vinegar, salt, and ginger in a large stockpot and bring to a boil over high heat. Reduce the heat a little and keep it at a boil for 10 minutes.

Stir in the pectin and bring it back to a boil. Cook for 2 to 3 minutes before you remove from the heat. Let cool to room temperature.

When cooled, stir in the lemon juice. Transfer the jelly to 2 (12-ounce) jars with lids and refrigerate for up to 3 weeks.

PEANUT-FIG RELISH

Serve with the Duck Sandwich and Bourbon-Raisin Slaw (page 159). It goes well with any game meat, and it's great on a holiday table alongside the ham. You can find dried figs at most grocery stores or online. SERVES 4 TO 6

2 cups dried Mission figs or any variety, quartered then the quarters halved

1 red bell pepper, stemmed, seeded, and finely diced

1 cup chopped roasted unsalted peanuts

2 shallots, finely diced

1 tablespoon finely minced cilantro

2 tablespoons honey

Zest and juice of 2 oranges

1 tablespoon rice wine vinegar

Kosher salt

Combine the figs with 2 cups water, or enough to just cover the figs, in a medium saucepan. Bring to a simmer over medium heat and cook until the water has evaporated.

Let the figs cool, then place them in a medium bowl and add all the remaining ingredients. Mix until well combined. Taste and more salt if needed. Chill for 2 hours before serving.

Refrigerate in an airtight container for up to 4 days.

CITRUS BRINE

Most people only use brines around holiday time for their turkeys, but there's so many more ways they can be used. Pork chops, a whole chicken before roasting, chicken wings before grilling, even duck breasts can all benefit from a minimum 2-hour brine. If you plan ahead, brining overnight always gives the best results. MAKES ABOUT 1 GALLON

½ cup kosher salt

½ cup soy sauce

¼ cup packed brown sugar

½ cup black peppercorns

3 garlic cloves, crushed

3 bay leaves

3 sprigs fresh thyme

2 sprigs fresh rosemary

1 orange, cut in half

1 lime, cut in half

1 lemon, cut in half

Pour 1 gallon of water in a large heavy-bottom stockpot. Add the salt, soy sauce, brown sugar, peppercorns, garlic, bay leaves, thyme, and rosemary and bring to a simmer over medium heat. Stir occasionally until the salt and brown sugar dissolve, about 5 minutes.

Remove from the heat and add the orange, lime, and lemon halves. Let stand for 30 to 40 minutes, until the mixture is cool. Then squeeze all the juice from the fruit into the brine and discard the fruit. The brine is ready to use, or you can refrigerate in an airtight container for up to 1 week before using.

VEGETABLE STOCK

This stock has a deep flavor that will enhance, soups, sauces, risottos and whatever else you like. The extra time it takes to make it is well worth it, but if you have to substitute store-bought, be sure to buy the low-sodium kind. MAKES 4 QUARTS

2 tablespoons extra-virgin olive oil

2 onions, coarsely chopped

½ pound mushrooms, cleaned

2 celery stalks, coarsely chopped

2 large carrots, coarsely chopped

1 bunch green onions, root end removed, and cut in half.

1 head garlic, ¼ inch cut off the top to expose the cloves

1 tomato, quartered

1 small apple, skin on, cored and sliced

1 bunch fresh parsley

3 bay leaves

1 tablespoon dried oregano

1 teaspoon peppercorns

1 tablespoon kosher salt

Heat the oil in an 8-quart stockpot over medium heat. Add the onions, mushrooms, and celery and sauté 15 minutes, or until lightly caramelized. Add the carrots, green onions, garlic, tomato, apple slices, parsley, bay leaves, oregano, peppercorns, salt, and 5 quarts of water and bring to a gentle boil. Reduce the heat to maintain a simmer, cover with a lid that is slightly vented, and cook for about 1 hour.

Strain the mixture into a large bowl through a fine-mesh strainer and let cool. When cool, pour into lidded containers or pint or quart jars, leaving 1-inch headroom for expansion. The stock can be stored, refrigerated, for up to 1 week, or frozen for up to 6 months.

D'S CHICKEN STOCK

Chicken stock is the backbone, or foundation, of countless recipes. Much like finding out who you are onstage, once you establish that, you can go into any subject matter and start to find your funny. If your chicken stock is good, whatever you use it for will taste even better.

MAKES ABOUT ½ GALLON

2 pounds chicken bones, from 2 (4-pound) chickens

2 large carrots, cut in 1-inch pieces (about 2 cups)

2 small onions, cut in 1-inch pieces (1½ to 2 cups)

3 celery stalks, cut in 1-inch pieces (about 1 cup)

8 thyme sprigs

4 garlic cloves

3 bay leaves

1 teaspoon black peppercorns

½ teaspoon kosher salt

Rinse the chicken bones in hot water for 3 to 4 minutes.

Combine all the ingredients and 1 gallon of water in a large stockpot or Dutch oven and bring to a boil over high heat. Reduce the heat to medium-low to simmer for 2 to 3 hours.

Pour the mixture through a fine-mesh strainer into a large bowl and discard all the solids. Let cool to room temperature. Refrigerate in an airtight container for up to 1 week, or freeze for up to 6 months.

BOURBON-SOAKED GOLDEN RAISINS

I always have these laying around for when I'm in the mood for a big salad or to add to a quick pan sauce with whatever protein I'm cooking. MAKES 3 PINTS

1 pound golden raisins

1½ cups bourbon or whiskey of choice

Combine the raisins, bourbon, and 3 cups of water in a large bowl and then divide between 3 pint-size mason jars, and refrigerate up to 1 month.

QUICK PRESERVED LEMONS

This is a great addition to fish or grilled vegetables, or on a salad, drizzled with olive oil.
MAKES 1 (8-OUNCE) JAR

4 lemons, wax scrubbed off

1 tablespoon kosher salt

1 teaspoon whole fennel seeds

½ teaspoon whole cumin seeds

2 tablespoons sugar

Dice the lemons, including the peel, and remove as many seeds as possible. Put the lemons and their juice in a bowl and sprinkle with the salt, fennel seeds, cumin seeds, and sugar. Toss well, transfer to an 8-ounce jar with a lid, and let sit at room temperature for at least 4 hours. Shake the jar periodically.

The preserved lemons can be served at this point, or refrigerated in an airtight container for 2 weeks.

CURED EGG

This condiment sounds fancy, but it is easy to make and can bring big flavor to all kinds of things—grate it over your favorite salad or on pasta dishes. Grated cured egg has the consistency of grated Parmesan cheese. MAKES 5 DRIED EGG YOLKS

1½ cups salt

1 cup sugar

1 teaspoon ground ginger

1 teaspoon pepper flakes

5 egg yolks

In a large bowl, whisk together the salt, sugar, ginger, and pepper flakes.

Place about ¾ cup of the mixture in the bottom of a glass dish. Make indentations in the mixture for the egg yolks using the back of a spoon. Lay the egg yolks in the indentations, being careful not to break them. Cover the eggs with the remaining salt mixture, seal the dish with plastic wrap or a tight cover, and refrigerate for 6 days.

Preheat the oven to 175 degrees F. Prepare a wire rack or pan with nonstick cooking spray.

Remove the eggs from the dish, brush off the curing mixture, gently rinse the yolks with water, and pat dry. Place the yolks on the prepared rack or pan and dry in the warm oven 1 hour. Allow to cool before grating.

Refrigerate in an airtight container for up to 3 weeks.

PICKLED CARROTS

If you love pickled vegetables and crunchy things but are tired of the average pickle, try these. And they are a good way to get in your daily vegetables! Serve them with Fennel-Braised Short Ribs (page 178). MAKES 1 (16-OUNCE) JAR

4 large carrots, cut into
  ¼-inch-thick julienne

3 cups white balsamic vinegar

1 cup orange juice

2 cups sugar

2 star anise pods

Place the julienned carrots in a large bowl.

In a large stockpot, combine the vinegar, orange juice, sugar, and star anise and bring to a boil over high heat.

Pour the hot liquid over the carrots. Allow to cool, then transfer the carrots and their liquid to an airtight container and refrigerate. These pickled carrots will be ready to eat in 1 day.

The pickled carrots can be stored in the refrigerator in a tightly covered container for up to 3 weeks.

TURMERIC-PICKLED CAULIFLOWER

Cauliflower turns up on more menus these days than French fries. It is found in some pizza crusts, there's frozen cauliflower rice in aisle six, and in 2015 it became popular as a "steak." For cauliflower aficionados, this is a new, but not gimmicky, quick-pickling way to enjoy this healthy vegetable. Serve with Pimento Cheese (page 82) and don't feel guilty about it!
MAKES 2 (16-OUNCE) JARS

1 head cauliflower, cut into florets

4 cups rice wine vinegar

1½ cups sugar

⅛ teaspoon kosher salt

½ teaspoon ground turmeric

2 tablespoons pickling spice

Place the cauliflower florets in a large glass bowl. Set aside.

In large stockpot, combine the vinegar, sugar, salt, turmeric, and pickling spice with 4 cups of water. Bring to a rapid boil over high heat. Once the brine is boiling, pour the mixture over the cauliflower florets and cover with a plate to keep florets submerged in the liquid.

Allow the liquid to cool, cover with plastic wrap, and refrigerate for up to 2 weeks.

PICKLED OKRA AND COLLARD GREEN STEMS

Remember those collard green stems you saved from the Mustard Green Chimichurri (page 54)? Use them here! These are a great way to get fiber with your pickles. MAKES 2 (16-OUNCE) JARS

½ pound okra (small tender pods)

½ pound collard green stems

4 garlic cloves, smashed

4 star anise pods

2 teaspoons fennel seeds

2 tablespoons pickling spice

1½ cups orange juice

1½ cups apple cider vinegar

1 teaspoon kosher salt

Prepare 2 jars with ring lids for pickling by handwashing in hot water or running them through a hot dishwasher cycle.

Split the okra and stems between the jars. In each jar, add 2 garlic cloves and 2 star anise pods. Divide the fennel seeds and pickling spice the same way.

In a large saucepan, prepare the pickling liquid by combining the orange juice, vinegar, and salt and bringing it to a boil over high heat.

Fill the jars with the hot liquid up to ¼ inch from the rim. Seal with the rings and lids on the jars.

You can eat them after 3 hours, but the longer they sit, the better they will taste. Refrigerate after opening.

PICKLED FRESNO PEPPERS AND SHALLOTS

This condiment is great with rich foods, like sausages, fried chicken, and burgers. I also use this quick pickle as a garnish on the Sautéed Royal Red Shrimp with Bourbon Maque Choux (page 136), and on the Berbere-Spiced Fried Chicken Sandwich (page 164). Note: if you'd like a milder pickle, slit the chiles lengthwise and remove their seeds before slicing.

MAKES 2 CUPS OR 1 (16-OUNCE) MASON JAR

1¼ cups apple cider vinegar

¼ cup orange juice

2 tablespoons brown sugar

1 teaspoon kosher salt

2 garlic cloves, sliced

3 sprigs thyme

1 tablespoon pickling spice

2 shallots, thinly sliced

½ pound Fresno peppers, thinly sliced

Combine the vinegar, orange juice, brown sugar, salt, garlic, thyme, and pickling spice in a small saucepan over medium-high heat and bring to a simmer.

Place the shallots and peppers in a 16-ounce mason jar, or a heatproof bowl Pour the hot mixture over the vegetables and allow to cool for at least 15 minutes before serving, or allow to cool completely and refrigerate in an airtight container for up to 1 month.

PICKLED GRAPES

I like to use this quick-pickling method on grapes, and I include them in all kinds of dishes. They make a great addition to any green salad, with the Pimento Cheese (page 82), or to top the Black-Eyed Pea Salad (page 103). Be creative with them! MAKES 2 CUPS

1 cup red seedless grapes, stemmed

1 cup green seedless grapes, stemmed

1 sprig rosemary

1 garlic clove, smashed

3 cups white balsamic vinegar

1½ cups sugar

1 teaspoon pickling spice

¼ teaspoon red pepper flakes

In a large bowl, combine the red and green grapes, rosemary, and garlic, mix well, and set aside.

In a large saucepan, combine the vinegar, sugar, pickling spice, and pepper flakes and bring to a boil over high heat, stirring until all the sugar is dissolved.

Pour the hot brine over the grapes and let them cool. Cut the grapes in half, lengthwise, before serving.

To store, transfer the grapes into a glass container with a lid and cover with the brine. They can be refrigerated for up to 3 weeks.

SPICED PECANS

These are great to have in your pantry, because they are a tasty addition to salads, make great game-day snacks, and are a good gift item for the holidays. (This last is from my inner Ina Garten!)

MAKES 2 CUPS

2 tablespoons chili powder

1 tablespoon ground ginger

1/2 teaspoon freshly ground black pepper

1/2 teaspoon garlic powder

1/2 teaspoon cayenne pepper

1 1/2 teaspoons ground cumin

1 tablespoon sugar

1 1/2 teaspoons kosher salt

1 1/2 teaspoons curry powder

2 cups pecan halves

1 tablespoon extra-virgin olive oil

Preheat the oven to 350 degrees F.

In a small bowl, combine the chili powder, ground ginger, pepper, garlic powder, cayenne, cumin, sugar, salt, and curry powder. Mix until well combined.

Reserve 3 teaspoons of the spice mix in a small bowl. (Store the remaining spice mix in an airtight container until ready to use in future recipes.)

In a medium bowl, combine the pecan halves and the olive oil. Dust the pecans with the reserved 3 teaspoons of spice mix, tossing to coat the pecans evenly.

Place the coated pecans in a single layer on a baking sheet and roast for 30 minutes, stirring once or twice, or until the pecans are a bronze color and the sugar in the spice mix is dissolved. Allow to cool before serving.

The spiced pecans can be stored at room temperature in an airtight container for up to 2 weeks.

OPEN-MIKERS

≡ APPETIZERS, SALADS, AND SOUPS ≡

PIMENTO CHEESE

Pimento cheese is a staple in any Southern kitchen. Some pimento cheeses are a little more savory, some a little more sweet or spicy. It can be eaten on just about anything you want—bread, crackers, or the vegetables of your choosing. At Southern National, we serve our pimento cheese on a platter with pickled cauliflower, radishes, sesame flatbread crackers, or whatever cracker you prefer. If you do not want to roast your own pepper, a small (4-ounce) jar of sliced pimientos, well drained, will work. SERVES 4 TO 6

1 red bell pepper, stemmed, and seeded

4 ounces (1 cup) grated
    sharp white cheddar

4 ounces (1 cup) grated sharp
    yellow cheddar

½ teaspoon garlic powder

½ teaspoon onion powder

½ teaspoon cayenne powder

1½ teaspoons Worcestershire sauce

½ cup Duke's mayonnaise

Preheat the broiler. Move the center rack to the top position in the oven if you don't have a broiler rack. Broil the bell pepper for 4 to 6 minutes, until the skin starts to blacken. Place the pepper in a bowl, cover with plastic wrap, and let sit for 10 minutes. Then remove the charred skin from the pepper and discard. Cut the pepper into slices.

Combine the grated cheese, garlic powder, onion powder, cayenne powder, Worcestershire sauce, mayonnaise, and bell pepper slices in a food processor and pulse until well combined.

Transfer to a bowl and serve chilled with your favorite bread, crackers, or vegetables. Pimento cheese can be refrigerated in an airtight container for up to 1 week.

PIMENTO CHEESE DEVILED EGGS

This could feed four people, but then again, it could just feed one if you love it like I do. Just saying. Pimento cheese makes almost everything it goes on taste better. But in this case, I think the addition of the egg yolk makes the cheese even better. MAKES ABOUT 2 CUPS, ENOUGH TO FILL 24 EGG HALVES

12 large eggs

4 tablespoons Duke's mayonnaise or your favorite brand

1 teaspoon apple cider vinegar

1½ tablespoons Dijon mustard

⅓ cup Pimento Cheese (page 82), at room temperature

⅛ teaspoon kosher salt

⅛ teaspoon freshly ground black pepper

¼ teaspoon paprika, for garnish

5 strips bacon, cooked crispy and crumbled, for garnish

Place the eggs in a large saucepan, add enough water to cover the eggs, and bring to a boil over high heat. Remove from the heat, cover the pan, and let stand for 10 minutes. The residual heat will finish cooking the eggs.

Fill a large bowl with ice and water to make an ice bath. Transfer the eggs to the ice bath to cool. Under running water, crack and peel the eggs, being careful not to tear the whites.

Cut the eggs in half lengthwise, remove the yolks, and transfer the yolks to a bowl. Add the mayonnaise, vinegar, and mustard, and mix until smooth and creamy. Fold in the pimento cheese, salt, and pepper and gently mix until incorporated.

Spoon or pipe the yolk mixture back in the whites. Garnish with a light dusting of paprika and some bacon crumbles.

. . . .

Note: 1 teaspoon of baking soda added to the boiling water will help the eggshell peel off easier.

HERBED GOAT CHEESE

This cheese can be served alone or as part of a cheese board or used in Grilled Okra and Shishito Peppers (page 115). MAKES ABOUT 1 POUND CHEESE

1 pound goat cheese, at
    room temperature

2 tablespoons minced chives

2 tablespoons minced parsley

Zest of 1 lemon

1 tablespoon minced mint

4 tablespoons half-and-half

1 teaspoon freshly ground black pepper

Place the goat cheese in the bowl of a stand mixer fitted with the whip attachment and add the chives, parsley, lemon zest, mint, half-and-half, and pepper. Whip for 3 to 5 minutes, until light and airy. Adjust the seasoning to taste, and serve at room temperature or chilled.

SONAT SMOKED FISH DIP

You can use any smoked fish for this recipe. My team and I came up with this snack to use up any ocean trout scraps we generated at the restaurant. But you can simply go out and buy some smoked trout—or salmon—and with little effort you'll have a quick snack to share with friends or an easy and unique potluck item. Serve with your favorite crackers or any flatbread.

SERVES 8 TO 10 AS AN APPETIZER

½ cup Duke's mayonnaise

4 ounces cream cheese

¼ cup small diced celery

1 tablespoon capers, drained and coarsely chopped.

1 teaspoon granulated onion

2 teaspoons hot sauce of your choice

1 teaspoon Worcestershire sauce

1 pound smoked trout or your favorite smoked fish

Kosher salt

Freshly ground black pepper

1 tablespoon finely chopped flat-leaf parsley, for garnish

In a large food processor, combine the mayonnaise, cream cheese, celery, capers, granulated onion, hot sauce, and Worcestershire sauce and purée until smooth. (Work in batches if you don't have a large food processor.)

If you picked up some smoked fish from the store, make sure you remove the skin and discard. Then break the fish into small pieces and remove any bones you may find.

Place the fish pieces in the food processor and pulse until the dip comes together into a thick spreadable consistency. Taste and add salt and pepper as needed. Transfer to a bowl and garnish with parsley.

JALAPEÑO HOE CAKES

Cornbread without the fuss—a kissing cousin to Johnny Cakes. The jalapeños add the needed spice.

MAKES 6 TO 8 (4-INCH) CAKES

1 cup all-purpose flour

1 cup yellow cornmeal

1 tablespoon baking powder

1 teaspoon kosher salt

1/4 teaspoon freshly ground
    black pepper

2 tablespoons sugar

2 eggs

1 cup whole milk

1/4 cup seeded and diced jalapeño
    peppers (about 3)

3 tablespoons melted butter

1 tablespoon butter, for the skillet

Pepper Jelly (page 67), for serving

Cane Syrup Butter (page 46),
    for serving

In a large bowl, mix together the flour, cornmeal, baking powder, salt, pepper, and sugar. Add the eggs and milk and mix well. It should be nice and thick. Then add the diced jalapeños and melted butter and stir to combine.

Grease a hot skillet or a griddle with butter and cook exactly like a pancake. Pour some batter on the skillet and cook for 2 minutes, wait for the bubbles to burst, then flip and cook 2 minutes more. Repeat with the rest of the batter.

Serve hot with the jelly and butter on the side.

CORN AND ANDOUILLE FRITTERS

This is one of those recipes that began as a staff meal on "fish fry" day. By adding sausage and crawfish, these corn fritters reach a new high. They go well with ice-cold beer and you can also dip them in the Cherry-Miso Sauce (page 61) or Comeback Sauce (page 55). For a change, serve these instead of hush puppies with your Uncle Bob's fried fish. SERVES 4

½ cup all-purpose flour

½ cup yellow cornmeal

1 teaspoon kosher salt, plus more for sprinkling

1 teaspoon baking powder.

¼ teaspoon cayenne pepper

½ cup whole milk

2 large eggs

¼ cup diced andouille sausage

¼ cup corn kernels, thawed if frozen

2 tablespoons melted butter

2 tablespoons thinly sliced green onion

½ cup drained and chopped crawfish tail meat

½ cup diced red pepper

4 cups vegetable oil, for frying

In a medium bowl, whisk together the flour, cornmeal, salt, baking powder, and cayenne pepper.

In a small bowl, whisk together the milk and eggs. Add the mixture to the dry ingredients, and stir to combine. Add the sausage, corn, melted butter, green onion, crawfish, and red pepper.

In a Dutch oven or a large heavy-bottom pot, heat the oil to 350 degrees F.

Use a tablespoon to drop the batter into the hot oil, trying not to overcrowd the pot. Fry in batches until golden brown, 2 to 3 minutes per side. Drain on paper towels, sprinkle with salt, and serve hot.

DUCK CONFIT BEIGNETS WITH CHERRY-MISO SAUCE

In France, anything that's fried is called a beignet. Here, we think of a beignet as a sweet, fried doughnut. Straddling those concepts, this recipe is essentially a cream puff dough (pâte à choux) with less sugar, and it's light and airy. It's a great way to feature the duck. SERVES 8

1 cup whole milk

½ cup (1 stick) unsalted butter

¼ teaspoon kosher salt, plus extra as needed

2 teaspoons sugar

1 cup all-purpose flour

4 large eggs

¼ cup chopped Duck Confit (page 124)

Zest of 1 orange

2 quarts vegetable oil, for frying

Cherry-Miso Sauce (page 61)

In a large saucepan over medium-high heat, combine the milk, butter, salt, and sugar. Bring to a boil, stirring to combine as the butter melts. Reduce the heat to medium and, using a wooden spoon, stir in the flour all at once.

Cook, stirring constantly for 1 minute, until the dough dries out slightly. This is key-excess moisture will cause your puffs to collapse. Remove the pan from the heat and let the dough cool for 5 minutes. Transfer the dough to a stand mixer.

Stir in the eggs 1 at a time until fully incorporated, before adding the next. (You can use a mixer, food processor, or a wooden spoon to get a workout. I like using the mixer because you can get a little air in the dough.)

Stir the duck meat and orange zest into the dough after the last egg is incorporated.

It is best if you can let the dough rest overnight, but you can cook immediately and still have a great result.

In a large heavy saucepan, Dutch oven, or deep fryer, heat the oil to 350 degrees F.

Working in batches, drop tablespoons of dough into the hot oil and cook 3 to 5 minutes until golden brown. Carefully remove the beignets using a wire skimmer and transfer to paper towels to drain.

Sprinkle with a little salt, and serve warm with the Cherry-Miso Sauce on the side.

MOM'S CORNBREAD

This is one of those recipes I will never forget. The first meal my mom taught me to make was red beans and rice along with this amazing cornbread—cooked in her fave 9-inch cast-iron pan. It's really good with the Sage Compound Butter (page 48). SERVES 6 TO 8

¼ cup vegetable oil (I use Wesson) plus more for the skillet

1 cup yellow cornmeal

1¼ cups all-purpose flour

2 tablespoons sugar, optional

1 teaspoon kosher salt

2 teaspoons baking powder

1 cup whole milk

1 egg

Butter, for serving

Preheat the oven to 425 degrees F.

Grease a 9-inch cast-iron skillet with some of the oil. Heat the greased skillet in the oven for about 5 minutes.

Sift the cornmeal, flour, sugar (if using), salt, and baking powder together in a large bowl. Add the milk, egg, and ¼ cup oil and mix well until the ingredients are just combined. Don't over mix.

Carefully remove the hot skillet from the oven and pour in the batter. Bake for 25 to 30 minutes, until the top is firm. The edges will be nicely browned.

Serve warm with butter on top.

Note: Croutons are so done—use stale or toasted crumbled cornbread on Caesar salads for a bit of crunch. Very tasty!

CRAB YELLOW RICE CAKE

I came up with this recipe to have another way to use leftover rice besides the old faithful fried rice or soup. My mentor, Darryl Evans, taught me this recipe, and I hope making these rice cakes makes you as happy as they make me every time I taste one. The combination of rice and crabmeat is a regional Southern tradition, and this is just one version of a classic dish. MAKES 4 CAKES

1 cup yellow rice, cooked according to package instructions, or 3 cups leftover Yellow Rice (page 118)

1 pound crabmeat, picked clean for any shell (claw meat is my preference)

2 tablespoons chopped green onion

1 tablespoon chopped flat-leaf parsley

1 tablespoon Dijon mustard

2 tablespoons mayonnaise

1 egg, beaten

1 tablespoon Worcestershire sauce

1 tablespoon Creole seasoning (I like Tony's Chachere's)

1 cup fine breadcrumbs

3 tablespoons olive oil

In a large bowl, combine the cooked rice with the crabmeat.

In a small bowl, combine the green onion, parsley, mustard, mayonnaise, egg, Worcestershire sauce, and Creole seasoning. Add it to the rice and crab and mix well. Form the mixture into 8 cakes.

Coat the cakes with breadcrumbs and refrigerate for 15 to 30 minutes before frying.

Heat the oil in a large heavy skillet over medium heat. Add the crab cakes and fry for 3 minutes on each side, until golden brown and crispy.

OYSTER BAKE

This easy appetizer gets a standing ovation every time I serve it! SERVES 4 TO 6

BREADCRUMBS

¾ cup panko breadcrumbs

¼ cup grated Parmesan cheese

1 tablespoon chopped fresh dill

½ teaspoon dried oregano

½ teaspoon garlic powder

OYSTERS

2 cups rock salt or uncooked
rice, for lining the pan

12 fresh oysters, scrubbed and
shucked on the half shell.

⅓ cup Mustard Green
Chimichurri (page 54)

¼ cup Smoked Paprika Compound Butter
(page 49), at room temperature

1 lemon, cut into wedges, as garnish

Preheat oven 425 degrees F.

To make the breadcrumbs, in a medium bowl, combine the breadcrumbs, Parmesan cheese, dill, oregano, and garlic powder. Mix well.

To make the oysters, pour a layer of rock salt or rice on a rimmed baking sheet. Place the shucked oysters on top of the salt. (I like to use the rock salt or rice as a bed because it keeps the oysters from tipping so they do not lose much juice when cooking.)

Top 6 of the oysters with 1 tablespoon chimichurri. Top the other 6 oysters with some of the soft paprika butter, then with some seasoned breadcrumbs. Bake the oysters for 8 to 10 minutes or until golden brown.

Serve with the lemon wedges on the side. Discard the rock salt or rice after use.

APPLE–CELERY ROOT SALAD

One of my fall favorites, I first developed this salad for a little market in Mobile that sold some of our food from Southern National. Unlike traditional coleslaw, this one is minus the mayonnaise, and it's a good addition to pork chops or grilled meat. SERVES 4 TO 6

1 medium celery root, peeled
    and julienned

1 fennel bulb, thinly sliced

1 Granny Smith apple, julienned (skin on)

2 Fresno peppers, seeded and julienned

2 teaspoons whole-grain mustard

Zest and juice of 1 lemon

1/3 cup extra-virgin olive oil

1 tablespoon chopped fresh parsley

1 teaspoon kosher salt

1 teaspoon freshly ground black pepper

In a large bowl, toss the celery root, fennel, apple, Fresno peppers, mustard, lemon zest and juice, olive oil, parsley, salt, and pepper together and mix well. Adjust the seasoning if needed.

The salad will keep, refrigerated, in an airtight container, for up to 1 week. It's actually better after the second day.

BOURBON-RAISIN SLAW

This is a vinaigrette slaw, not a mayonnaise-based slaw. The addition of the Bourbon-Soaked Golden Raisins (page 72) adds a sassy taste to an otherwise sober dish. This slaw is ready to party! MAKES ABOUT 12 CUPS

SLAW

1 head green cabbage, finely shredded

1 large carrot, grated

1 tablespoon Bourbon-Soaked Golden Raisins (page 72)

1/2 yellow onion, thinly sliced

DRESSING

1/2 cup apple cider vinegar

1 shallot, coarsely chopped

1/2 tablespoon whole-grain mustard

1 tablespoon honey

2 tablespoons Bourbon-Soaked Golden Raisins (page 72), with some of the liquid

1 1/2 cups extra-virgin olive oil

1 teaspoon kosher salt

1 teaspoon freshly ground black pepper

To make the slaw, toss together the cabbage, carrot, soaked raisins, and onion in a large bowl.

To make the dressing, in a blender, combine the vinegar, shallot, mustard, honey, and soaked raisins. As you run the blender on low speed, slowly drizzle in the oil. If your mixture starts to get too thick, blend in some of the bourbon liquid from the soaking raisins to get your desired consistency. Season with salt and pepper, taste, and adjust if needed.

Add half the dressing to the cabbage mixture and gently toss. Slowly add more dressing until you reach your desired consistency.

Store the slaw in the refrigerator, in an airtight container for up to 5 days.

GOLDEN BEET AND ARUGULA SALAD WITH PICKLED GRAPES AND SPICED PECANS

If you've already made the Pickled Grapes (page 78) and the Spiced Pecans (page 79), this salad will be a breeze to compose and is very impressive on a table. SERVES 4 TO 6

8 small golden beets, scrubbed

1 tablespoon kosher salt

3 bunches arugula, washed, dried, and stems removed

1 cup Pickled Grapes (page 78)

¼ cup (about 2 medium) thinly sliced radishes

1 cup Spiced Pecans (page 79)

Buttermilk Dressing (page 53)

Place the beets in a medium stockpot with enough water to cover. Add the salt and bring to a simmer over medium heat. Simmer for 40 minutes, or until the beets are fork tender. Add more water as needed during the cooking to keep the beets covered. Allow the beets to cool, then peel and cut into 1-inch cubes.

To serve, place the arugula in a serving bowl or on a platter. Top with the golden beets, Pickled Grapes, sliced radishes, and Spiced Pecans. Pass the Buttermilk Dressing at the table.

BLACK-EYED PEA SALAD

Whenever I mix together this combo of ingredients I think about my mentor, Chef Evans. When I was about 20 years old, he made a black-eyed pea relish for a pork tenderloin dish that I tasted, and it was the first time I realized the humble food I grew up eating could be served in an elevated setting. I didn't know it then, but it would define who I am as a cook today. With the red peppers, yellow peppers, red onion, goat cheese, and aged balsamic vinaigrette, this is every fresh thing you ever wanted in a bowl, and more. So when I make this salad at home or at work, it's because I'm thinking of Chef Evans, someone I lost and miss very much. SERVES 4

SALAD

2 tablespoons extra-virgin olive oil

1 tablespoon peeled and coarsely chopped fresh ginger

1 (15-ounce) can black-eyed peas, drained and rinsed

2 teaspoons kosher salt

1/4 teaspoon freshly ground black pepper

1/2 bunch fresh flat-leaf parsley, chopped

1 yellow pepper, seeded, and diced

1 red pepper, seeded, and diced

1/2 red onion, diced

1 (5-ounce) package arugula

1/4 cup sunflower seeds, for garnish

1 cup goat cheese, for garnish

VINAIGRETTE DRESSING

1/4 cup aged balsamic vinegar

1 cup extra-virgin olive oil

1 tablespoon whole-grain mustard

To make the salad, in a medium saucepan over medium heat, combine the olive oil and ginger and sauté for 2 to 3 minutes, until the ginger becomes slightly brown. Stir in the black-eyed peas, salt, and pepper, and reduce the heat to a simmer just long enough to warm throughout. Set the pan aside and let the beans cool to room temperature.

Using a slotted spoon, scoop the cooled beans into a bowl. Add the chopped parsley, the yellow and red peppers, and the onion and mix well. Adjust the seasoning as needed.

To make the dressing, combine the vinegar, olive oil, and mustard in a jar or a pint container with a lid. Seal and shake well. You will have enough dressing for four salads.

To serve, divide the arugula between four plates, then equally portion the black-eyed pea mixture among the servings, placing on top of the greens. Sprinkle the sunflower seeds and some goat cheese on top. Add a few spoonfuls of the vinaigrette over each salad.

FENNEL, SUMMER SAUSAGE, AND APRICOT SALAD WITH ROSEMARY VINAIGRETTE

You can make this salad year-round using dried apricots, but when the fruit is in season, there is nothing better than slicing up fresh apricots. Both versions are tasty. SERVES 6

SALAD

2 large fennel bulbs, cores removed

2 shallots

¼ cup pecan pieces, toasted

6 dried apricots, cut into thin strips

½ teaspoon kosher salt

½ teaspoon freshly ground
   black pepper

8 to 10 slices summer sausage,
   cut into strips

ROSEMARY VINAIGRETTE

4 tablespoons finely chopped
   fresh rosemary

2 teaspoons minced garlic

1 tablespoon Dijon mustard

¼ cup rice wine vinegar

½ cup extra-virgin olive oil

¼ teaspoon freshly ground
   black pepper

¼ teaspoon kosher salt

To make the salad, using a mandoline or a sharp knife, shave the fennel and shallots as thinly as possible and place them in a large bowl. Add the pecans, apricots, salt, pepper, and sausage and mix well.

To make the vinaigrette, combine the rosemary, garlic, mustard, vinegar, olive oil, pepper, and salt in a glass jar with a lid. Seal and shake really well until emulsified.

Toss the salad with just enough vinaigrette to suit yourself. Serve immediately.

SMOKED TROUT POTATO SALAD

One of the early salads I came up with when I was the chef at the One Flew South was created as a way to highlight the Georgia trout, a Southern ingredient that I could get easily from a local vendor. When I worked on creating this recipe, I had to "smuggle" the fish past security in order to get it into the kitchen because the airport didn't allow vendors to bring their food in through security checkpoints. Now I like to use packaged smoked trout because it makes the preparation quick and easy. SERVES 4

DRESSING

¼ cup Duke's mayonnaise

½ cup sour cream

½ cup buttermilk

1 tablespoon lime juice

1 teaspoon granulated garlic

⅛ teaspoon cayenne pepper

1 teaspoon kosher salt

1 teaspoon freshly ground black pepper

SALAD

1 (8-ounce) package smoked trout, skin removed, and broken into bite-size pieces

1 pound fingerling potatoes, blanched and cut in half

½ cup fresh peas, blanched (or frozen peas, if you can't get fresh)

¼ bunch flat-leaf parsley, coarsely chopped

⅓ cup fresh dill

⅓ cup torn fresh mint leaves

1 shallot, shaved on a mandoline

2 tablespoons extra-virgin olive oil

2 hard-boiled eggs, peeled and cut into 4 wedges

To make the dressing, stir together the mayonnaise, sour cream, buttermilk, lime juice, garlic, and cayenne pepper in a medium bowl. Taste and add salt and pepper.

To make the salad, in a large bowl toss together the trout, potatoes, peas, parsley, dill, mint, shallot, and olive oil. Divide the mixture onto plates, drizzle with the dressing, and top off with the eggs.

Notes: To blanch the peas, cook them in boiling water for 30 seconds to 2 minutes, until they float to the top.

You aren't required to plate this dish, that's just how I conceived it for the restaurant. You can serve it from a large decorative serving bowl for a home dinner party, or chilled on ice for a tailgate party. If you can get your hands on some pea tendrils that would be a nice touch.

LENTIL AND CHICKPEA SALAD

This cold protein-and-fiber-packed salad will keep up to one week in the refrigerator. It's a hearty dish with a nutty flavor that's great paired with roasted chicken, fish, or served as a vegetarian option for lunch or dinner. It's perfect for an outdoor cookout, too. SERVES 6 TO 10

2 cups French green lentils (found at most grocery stores)

3 bay leaves

5 sprigs thyme

2 teaspoons kosher salt, divided

2 medium carrots, peeled and cut in half

4 tablespoons extra-virgin olive oil

¼ teaspoon freshly ground black pepper

1 (15-ounce) can chickpeas, drained and rinsed

2 garlic cloves, finely chopped

¼ cup minced fresh flat-leaf parsley

⅓ cup coarsely chopped fresh mint

1 small red onion, diced

¼ cup diced red bell pepper

5 tablespoons lemon juice

In a medium saucepan, combine the lentils, bay leaves, thyme, and 1 teaspoon salt. Add enough water to cover by 1 inch and bring to a boil over high heat. Reduce the heat to medium-low and simmer, uncovered, for 15 to 20 minutes, or until the lentils are tender but not mushy. Drain the lentils and discard the bay leaves and thyme sprigs. Set aside.

To grill the carrots, heat a grill or grill pan on medium until hot, 5 to 10 minutes.

While the grill heats, toss the carrot halves in the olive oil and season with the remaining 1 teaspoon salt and pepper. Grill the carrots for 20 to 25 minutes until lightly charred. Set aside to cool, then cut the halves into ¼-inch pieces.

In a large bowl, place the lentils, carrot pieces, chickpeas, garlic, parsley, mint, onion, bell pepper, and lemon juice and toss to combine. Adjust the seasoning as needed. Serve chilled, or at room temperature.

CAULIFLOWER AND PARSNIP SOUP

This soup is so soulful and delicious, it is creamily unctuous—and by this, I mean flattering, not oily! It can be made with vegetable stock if you want it to be vegetarian. It is meant to be a thick, creamy soup, but if you want to adjust the consistency, use extra chicken stock to do so.

SERVES 6 TO 8

2 teaspoons canola oil

2 teaspoons unsalted butter

½ large sweet onion, diced

2 stalks celery, diced

2 garlic cloves, sliced

1 teaspoon ground cumin

1 bay leaf

3 tablespoons chopped
   fresh thyme, divided

1 cup white wine

3 cups peeled and diced parsnips

1 head cauliflower, chopped

3 cups heavy cream

8 cups D's Chicken Stock (page 71)
   or store-bought, divided

1 tablespoon kosher salt

2 teaspoons freshly ground
   black pepper

1 teaspoon white balsamic vinegar

In a large stockpot over medium-high heat, combine the oil and butter, and heat until the butter melts. Add the onion, celery, and garlic and cook for 3 to 5 minutes, until soft and translucent. Next add the cumin, bay leaf, and 1 tablespoon fresh thyme, stirring to combine. Add the white wine and deglaze and cook until the liquid is reduced by half.

Add the parsnips, cauliflower, cream, and 5 cups chicken stock. Lower the heat to medium and cook for 35 to 40 minutes until the vegetables are tender.

Remove the bay leaf. Transfer the soup to a food processor and purée the mixture for 2 to 3 minutes, until smooth. You may need to do this in batches. Season with the salt, pepper, and balsamic vinegar, adjusting amounts to taste. Add the remaining 3 cups chicken stock to bring the soup to your desired consistency, and cook over medium heat for 3 to 5 minutes until the soup is warmed through. Garnish with the remaining fresh thyme and serve warm.

WHITE BEAN SOUP WITH KALE AND CHICKEN SAUSAGE

This is a hearty wintertime soup. Navy beans (another name for white beans) are my favorite. My uncle used to cook these beans on a barbecue grill, so they had a smoky flavor—I was hooked. You can also cook these beans in a Dutch oven or on a Green Egg grill. Crack the lid open a little, and the beans will take on that smoky flavor. SERVES 6 TO 8

3 (15-ounce) cans navy beans, drained and rinsed, divided

5 cups D's Chicken Stock (page 71) or store-bought, divided

2 tablespoons extra-virgin olive oil

1 pound chicken sausage, sliced

1 cup diced onion

½ cup diced carrot

½ cup diced celery

4 garlic cloves, sliced

1 tablespoon fresh rosemary, minced

1 pound baby potatoes, scrubbed and quartered, skin on

2 teaspoons kosher salt

2 teaspoons freshly ground black pepper

2 cups coarsely chopped kale

1 tablespoon minced fresh chives

¼ cup freshly grated Parmesan cheese

Crusty bread, optional

Combine 1 can of beans and 1 cup chicken stock in a blender or food processor. Blend until smooth.

Place the remaining beans in a bowl and set them aside.

Heat the oil in a large Dutch oven over medium heat. Add the chicken sausage and cook, stirring constantly, for 3 to 5 minutes, until it is slightly brown. Add the onion, carrot, and celery and cook, stirring occasionally, for 7 to 8 minutes, until the veggies are softened.

Stir in the garlic and rosemary and cook, stirring constantly, for about 30 seconds, until the soup becomes fragrant.

Add the blended beans, drained beans, potatoes, and the remaining 4 cups chicken stock. Season with salt and pepper, and simmer, uncovered, over medium-low heat for 25 to 30 minutes, until the vegetables are tender.

Stir in the kale and simmer for a few minutes until the kale starts to wilt. Stir in the chives and serve hot with grated Parmesan cheese and some crusty bread, if using.

BIT PARTS

≡ SIDE DISHES ≡

GRILLED OKRA AND SHISHITO PEPPERS

This dish is cooked on an outdoor grill (you will need a grill basket), which makes it a great summer addition to whatever meat you're grilling that day. Okra and peppers go well with fish, fowl, or game. SERVES 8

½ pound okra

½ pound shishito peppers

4 tablespoons extra-virgin olive oil

2 teaspoons kosher salt

2 teaspoons freshly ground black pepper

Herbed Goat Cheese (page 86)

Pickled Carrots (page 74)

Jazzed-Up Hoisin Sauce (page 55)

Cured Egg (page 73)

Preheat a grill or grill plate, if you don't have an outdoor grill. Place the grill basket directly on the grill.

In a large bowl, use tongs to toss together the okra, shishito peppers, olive oil, salt, and pepper.

Place the seasoned okra and peppers in the basket on the hot grill and cook 7 to 10 minutes, until the okra and peppers are tender and have some serious char marks. Halfway through the cooking time, give the okra and peppers a quick toss to evenly grill them.

Remove from the grill and let them come room temperature before plating them with the goat cheese, Pickled Carrots, Jazzed-Up Hoisin Sauce, and Cured Egg.

CREAMED COLLARD GREENS

If you like creamed spinach, you'll love this dish. After being cooked in cream for just a short time, the collards lose any bitterness and reveal a grassy, nutty taste. Make sure you save the stems to make Pickled Okra and Collard Green Stems (page 76)! SERVES 6 TO 8

3 bunches collard greens, stemmed, and cut into ½-inch pieces

2 tablespoons plus 1 teaspoon salt, divided

2 tablespoons extra-virgin olive oil

1 large yellow onion

5 garlic cloves, thinly sliced

2 bay leaves

4 Fresno peppers, seeded and julienned

1 tablespoon chopped fresh ginger

2 teaspoons smoked paprika

1 teaspoon ground coriander

3 to 4 cups diced butternut squash (about 1 medium squash)

1 teaspoon freshly ground black pepper

1 cup D's Chicken Stock (page 71) or Vegetable Stock (page 70) or store-bought

2 cups heavy cream

Zest and juice of 1 lemon, for garnish

2 tablespoons chopped fresh flat-leaf parsley, for garnish

To blanch the collard greens, bring a large pot of water to a boil over high heat and season with 2 tablespoons salt. When the water is boiling, drop the greens in and cook for 3 to 4 minutes until bright green. Immediately drain the collards in a colander and rinse with cold water. Set aside while you prepare the rest of the recipe.

Heat the oil in a large Dutch oven over medium heat. When the oil starts to shimmer, toss in the onion, garlic, bay leaves, peppers, ginger, smoked paprika, coriander, squash, the remaining 1 teaspoon salt, and the pepper and cook, stirring occasionally, for 2 to 3 minutes. Stir in the stock and continue cooking for 5 to 6 minutes, or until the onion and squash are tender and the stock is almost gone.

Reduce the heat to medium-low, add the cream and cook until it reduces by half. Stir in the blanched greens and cook until the collards are just warmed through. Stir in the lemon juice. Taste and adjust the seasoning. Serve hot, garnished with a sprinkle of lemon zest and chopped parsley.

BOURBON MAQUE CHOUX

This is one of those classic southern Louisiana side dishes, which is an elevated creamed corn. It's often cooked in bacon fat, though here I've opted for olive oil and butter. Over the years I have refined my own version of this beloved dish, with the addition of bourbon really setting it apart. When I make Sautéed Royal Red Shrimp (page 136), I like to cook this in the same pan that was used to sear the shrimp, to get all that added flavor. SERVES 4

1 tablespoon extra-virgin olive oil

1 tablespoon butter

4 cobs corn, shucked, kernels removed, and milk from the cob reserved (see Note)

½ onion, cut into small dice

2 garlic cloves, sliced

1 red bell pepper, cut into small dice

1 jalapeño pepper, seeded, and cut into small dice

1 teaspoon Creole seasoning (I prefer Tony Chachere's)

¼ teaspoon kosher salt

¼ teaspoon freshly ground black pepper

1 ounce bourbon of choice

¼ cup shrimp stock or D's Chicken Stock (page 71) or store-bought

2 cups heavy cream

½ teaspoon chopped fresh cilantro

½ teaspoon chopped fresh parsley

Heat the oil and butter in a skillet or large saucepan over medium heat. Add the corn and onion and sauté for 10 minutes until the vegetables are tender and slightly browned. Add the garlic, bell pepper, and jalapeño and sauté for 5 minutes. Season with the Creole seasoning, salt, and pepper and stir. Add the bourbon and stir to deglaze the skillet. Reduce the heat to low, add the stock, heavy cream, and reserved corn milk and simmer until the sauce slightly thickens.

Toss in the cilantro and parsley, and adjust the seasoning as needed.

Note: To prepare the corn, first remove it from the cob by using a knife to cut down along side of each cob, rotating until all of the kernels are removed. Next, extract the milk from the cob—you don't waste any part of the sweet corn. To do this, after removing the kernels, set the cob on a rimmed plate and run the back of your knife along the cob. With a little pressure, the natural milk will be released.

YELLOW RICE

This really easy yellow rice recipe can complement just about any meal and can be made in a rice cooker or on the stovetop. I first went down the yellow-rice rabbit hole after finding out from a doctor that turmeric was good for inflammation (this was long before it hit the mainstream) and I never went back. I like to toast the rice in some butter before boiling to give it an amazing flavor. You can skip this step if you want to, but I wouldn't if I were you. MAKES ABOUT 3 CUPS

3 tablespoons butter

1 cup Carolina Gold rice or
    other long-grain rice

1 medium onion, cut into fine dice

2 garlic cloves, cut into slices

2 bay leaves

1 teaspoon ground turmeric, or
    ½ teaspoon yellow curry powder

1 teaspoon ground coriander

1 teaspoon smoked paprika

½ teaspoon kosher salt

¼ teaspoon freshly ground
    black pepper

2 cups D's Chicken Stock
    (page 71) or Vegetable Stock
    (page 70) or store-bought

Heat the butter in a large saucepan over medium heat. Add the rice and diced onion, and gently stir until the onion is lightly browned. Add the garlic, bay leaves, turmeric, coriander, smoked paprika, salt, and pepper and stir until well combined.

Slowly stir in the stock, increase the heat to medium-high, and bring to a boil. Reduce the heat to low, cover the pot, and simmer for 20 to 25 minutes. Remove from the heat and fluff with a fork.

YELLOW RICE AND BOK CHOY HOPPIN' JOHN

Hoppin' John is a Southern classic, and there are thousands of variations. This makes it one-thousand-and-one. SERVES 4 TO 6

2 cups dried field peas

2 tablespoons extra-virgin olive oil

2 shallots, julienned

2 baby bok choy, ½ inch removed from the bottom and patted dry

3 cups Yellow Rice (page 118)

1 teaspoon kosher salt

½ teaspoon freshly ground black pepper

3 cups D's Chicken Stock (page 71) or store-bought

1 tablespoon chopped flat-leaf parsley

Cook the field peas according to the package directions and set aside.

In a Dutch oven over medium-high heat, combine the oil, shallots, and bok choy and sauté for 3 minutes until the bok choy is wilted.

Add the rice, salt, pepper, stock, and cooked field peas and mix well. Lower the heat to maintain a simmer and cook for 5 minutes, until the ingredients are warmed through. Garnish with the chopped parsley and serve.

GARLIC RICE

I like to serve this rice with Creamed Collard Greens (page 116), and Kentuckyaki Drumsticks (page 160). SERVES 6 TO 8

2 tablespoons butter

2 tablespoons extra-virgin olive oil

8 garlic cloves, cut into slices

2 cups Carolina Gold rice or another long-grain rice

4 cups D's Chicken Stock (page 71) or Vegetable Stock (page 70) or store-bought

2 teaspoons chopped fresh flat-leaf parsley

Heat the butter and olive oil in a saucepan over medium heat. Add the garlic and cook 1 to 2 to minutes.

Stir in the rice and cook 4 minutes, stirring occasionally to make sure rice doesn't stick, until the rice becomes slightly translucent. The rice may brown slightly due to the butter, which is great—it will give a nutty flavor to the finished rice.

Stir in the stock and bring to a boil. Reduce the heat to medium-low, cover, and cook 20 to 25 minutes. Carefully remove the lid, fluff the rice with a fork, and garnish with chopped parsley before serving.

MUSTARD GREEN, LEEK, AND CREAM POTATO HASH

This hash goes well with so many main dishes, and it will keep, refrigerated, for up to 4 days. For those nights you don't want to cook, enjoy any leftovers of this hash with a store-bought deli chicken and a bottle of white wine. SERVES 4 TO 6

2 teaspoons salt

1 large russet potato, peeled, diced in ¼-inch cubes

1 turnip, peeled, diced in ¼-inch cubes

2 tablespoons extra-virgin olive oil

1 leek, trimmed and diced

2 garlic cloves, thinly sliced

1 cup D's Chicken Stock (page 71) or store-bought

1 tablespoon Creole mustard

1 cup heavy cream

4 sprigs thyme, stems discarded

Zest of 1 lemon

4 turnip green leaves, coarsely chopped

⅛ teaspoon kosher salt

⅛ teaspoon freshly ground black pepper

Combine the salt and 4 cups water in a stockpot and bring to boil over medium-high heat. Add the diced potato and turnip and blanch for 5 minutes.

Drain the potato and turnip in a colander, place them on a rimmed baking sheet, and refrigerate until cool.

Heat the oil in a large cast-iron skillet over medium heat. Add the leek and sauté 6 to 8 minutes, until it starts to slightly melt.

Stir in the blanched potato and turnip, garlic, stock, and mustard. Reduce the heat to maintain a simmer and cook for 5 minutes, stirring occasionally, until the stock is reduced by half. Mix in the heavy cream, thyme, and lemon zest and cook for 1 minute more.

Add the turnip greens and cook, stirring, for another 5 minutes, until the leaves are wilted and the potatoes and turnips are tender. Season with salt and pepper.

DUCK CONFIT HASH

I loved corned beef hash with toast and coffee when I was a kid. I thought about that treat when I came up with this duck recipe. The little pieces of duck get crispy when you are pan-frying the hash, which is really flavorful. You will need quite a bit of duck fat and you can get it and the duck itself from a local international food market or online. The process of slowly cooking the duck and adding the fat is an old technique, which preserves the meat and adds to the flavor, and the duck is generally stored in the fat until it's used in a recipe.

There are lots of ways to serve this hash, but my favorite is in a bowl topped with an over-easy egg and a little hot sauce. This is a showy dish that works well for a brunch party, served in a large dish with the fried eggs on top. The yolks make a great sauce.

The duck needs to marinate overnight and then cook in a low oven for five-plus hours, so be sure to plan ahead when making this recipe. I assure you it's well worth the time. SERVES 4 TO 6

DUCK CONFIT

6 duck legs

1½ cups kosher salt

1½ cups brown sugar

3 garlic cloves, finely minced, and with ½ teaspoon kosher salt crushed into a paste

1 tablespoon grated fresh ginger

½ teaspoon ground bay leaf

1 tablespoon finely chopped fresh thyme

1½ teaspoons Worcestershire sauce

1½ teaspoon freshly ground black pepper

4 quarts duck fat

To confit the duck legs, begin by trimming off any excess fat and pat the legs dry. Place them on a baking sheet and set aside.

In a small bowl, combine the salt, brown sugar, garlic paste, ginger, bay leaf, thyme, Worcestershire sauce, and pepper. Season the duck legs liberally with this spice mixture, rubbing it into the flesh side of the leg. Return the legs to the baking sheet, cover with plastic wrap, and refrigerate overnight to marinate.

The next day, remove the duck from the refrigerator and let come to room temperature.

Preheat the oven to 200 degrees F.

Pour the duck fat into a large oven-safe saucepan or Dutch oven over medium heat and warm the fat. When hot, but not boiling, add the duck legs to the pan, lower the heat to medium-low, and slowly heat until you see a single bubble form. Cover the pan, transfer to the oven, and cook for 5 hours, or until the meat is fork tender and the duck fat is clear.

Let the duck cool. Pull the meat from the bones and set it aside in a bowl until you are ready to make hash. Discard all the bones.

HASH

3 tablespoons vegetable oil

2 cups shiitake mushrooms, stems removed and julienned

4 sweet potatoes, diced into ½-inch pieces, and blanched

2 shallots, julienned

½ teaspoon grated fresh ginger

1 teaspoon kosher salt

½ teaspoon freshly ground black pepper

½ cup D's Chicken Stock (page 71) or store-bought

1 tablespoon chopped fresh flat-leaf parsley

Juice of 1 lemon

3 green onions, thinly sliced

¼ cup Jazzed-Up Hoisin Sauce (page 55)

6 large eggs, cooked over easy, for serving

To make the duck hash, warm the oil in a large skillet over medium-high heat. Add the mushrooms and sweet potatoes and cook for 7 to 8 minutes until the potatoes and mushrooms start to get a little color. Add the shallots and ginger and season with salt and pepper. Cook for 2 to 3 minutes, stirring to incorporate the ingredients.

Reduce the heat to medium-low, add the duck meat, and cook another 2 to 3 minutes. At this time, the potatoes should be releasing some starch and starting to stick to the pan. Add the stock and deglaze the pan by scraping up all the browned goodness on the bottom of the pan with a spoon. When the stock has just about evaporated, turn off the heat and stir in the parsley, lemon juice, green onions, and hoisin sauce until well combined.

Serve immediately, accompanied by an over-easy egg.

COCONUT CREAM CORN AND POTATOES

When I was a kid, one of my favorite afternoon snacks I made myself was heating up a can of creamed corn with a sliced hot dog in it. This is my grownup version of a favorite. SERVES 8 TO 10

2 tablespoons extra-virgin olive oil

1 medium onion, diced

4 garlic cloves, sliced

1 red bell pepper, diced

2 jalapeños, seeded and diced

1 celery rib, diced

6 ears of corn, kernels removed from cob (about 4 cups canned corn, drained, or frozen)

½ pound baby potatoes, cut into quarters

1 teaspoon kosher salt

1 teaspoon freshly ground black pepper

1 teaspoon ground coriander

1 (13.5-ounce) can coconut milk

1 cup Vegetable Stock (page 70)

1 tablespoon Creole mustard

2 tablespoons chopped parsley, for garnish

2 tablespoons chopped chives, for garnish

In a large skillet or Dutch oven over medium-high heat, combine the oil, onion, garlic, bell pepper, jalapeño, and celery. Sauté for 5 minutes, stirring occasionally, until the vegetables are soft and the onion is translucent.

Stir in the corn and potatoes, and season with salt, pepper, and coriander. Sauté for 2 minutes, then stir in the coconut milk, stock, and mustard. Reduce the heat to medium-low and simmer 6 to 8 minutes, or until the potatoes are tender. Serve, garnished with the chopped parsley and chives.

Note: The mustard will act as a thickening agent, so you may need to add a little more stock if it's too thick for your liking.

POTATO GNOCCHI (POTATO DUMPLINGS)

Some folks like to roast their potatoes for a classic gnocchi preparation, but as a cook you learn who you are and where you come from through the repetition of cooking. I found when I boiled the potato instead of roasting it, I was able to introduce the flavor of bay leaves, which is one of the foundation flavor bombs in my mother's cooking. Thanks, Mom! And these gnocchi work really well with my Cornmeal-Dusted Trout (page 141). SERVES 4

1 pound Yukon Gold potatoes, skin on

4 bay leaves

1 egg yolk

¼ teaspoon kosher salt

¼ cup 00 flour (fine-grade Italian flour), or all-purpose flour, plus more as needed

Rice flour, for dusting

Fill a stockpot with water and boil the potatoes with the bay leaves over medium-high heat for 25 to 30 minutes until tender. Pierce a potato with a small knife to check for doneness; if the knife slips out with ease, the potatoes are ready. Drain the potatoes and dry well (moisture and gnocchi do not get along).

Once cool enough to handle, peel off the skins. Pass the potatoes through a potato ricer over a large wide bowl. Allow the steam to evaporate. The potatoes should be warm to the touch. If the potatoes are dry enough, you won't need extra flour later on.

Form a well in the center of the potatoes. Add the egg yolk and salt, and sprinkle some of the flour on top. Using a fork, gently mix a few times to combine, gradually adding the rest of the flour as you go. Once the dough starts to stick, finish by hand.

Bring the dough together to form a ball (think of it as smashing the dough together, not kneading it, as you would if making pasta). It should feel like a big warm mashed potato ball. If it's sticky, add a little more flour. Cover with a cloth and let rest for 10 to 15 minutes. This will make the dough easier to roll.

Cut the dough ball into 4 equal pieces. Roll one piece into a 10- to 12-inch-long log. Cut the log crosswise into 20 to 22 (½-inch-wide) gnocchi. (They will look like little pillows.) Dust a baking sheet with rice flour, which will keep the gnocchi from sticking. Transfer the gnocchi to the baking sheet. Repeat with the rest of the dough.

To cook, bring a stock pot of salted water (As the chef who showed me how to make this recipe told me, your water should taste like the ocean.) to a boil. Working in batches, cook the gnocchi for about 1 minute. When they float to the top of the pot, they're ready. Transfer the gnocchi to a bowl with a slotted spoon, or directly into a sauce of choice.

MOJO POTATOES

The Mojo Sauce takes these humble roasted potatoes to an entirely new flavor level. The bay leaves add the flavor of my Louisiana home. It adds a lovely aroma and an herbaceous flavor that deepens the flavor of the dish. SERVES 4 TO 6

2 pounds baby potatoes,
    skin on, scrubbed

3 bay leaves

2 teaspoons kosher salt

Spray olive oil

¼ cup unsalted butter, melted

½ teaspoon freshly ground
    black pepper

½ cup SoNat Mojo Sauce (page 59)

2 teaspoons chopped fresh
    flat-leaf parsley

Preheat the oven to 425 degrees F.

In a large pot filled with water, boil the potatoes with the bay leaves and salt for 5 to 10 minutes, until fork tender. Drain the potatoes and set aside to cool for 5 to 10 minutes.

Line a baking sheet with parchment paper and lightly spray with olive oil. Place the boiled potatoes on the baking sheet about 3 inches apart. Gently smash each potato with a fork until they are flattened to about ½-inch thick.

Brush each potato generously with the melted butter and sprinkle them with pepper. Bake for 15 to 20 minutes, or until the potatoes are golden brown and crispy to your liking.

Transfer the potatoes to a bowl, add the mojo sauce, and toss until the potatoes are coated with the sauce.

Garnish with chopped parsley and serve. Adjust the seasoning if you like by adding more sauce, salt, or pepper.

ROASTED POTATOES WITH PECAN-BASIL PESTO

These potatoes taste amazing: think potato gnocchi in pesto sauce, but with a crunch. I like to serve this as a side dish with seafood or with a summer grill. SERVES 6 TO 8

3 pounds russet potatoes, peeled

2 teaspoons kosher salt

2 teaspoons white pepper

2 bay leaves

5 sprigs thyme

¼ cup extra-virgin olive oil

3 tablespoons Pecan-Basil Pesto (page 56)

Preheat the oven to 400 degrees F. Line a baking sheet with aluminum foil.

Cut the potatoes into even-size pieces a little smaller than a golf ball. Rinse the potatoes in cold water to remove the extra starch. Place the potatoes in a large pot with just enough water to cover by 2 inches.

Add the salt, white pepper, bay leaves, and thyme and bring to a boil over high heat. Reduce the heat to medium and cook for 10 to 15 minutes. Drain the potatoes in a strainer and let them dry for 5 to 10 minutes.

While the potatoes are drying, discard the bay leaves and thyme.

Give the potatoes a gentle shake in the strainer to rough them up a bit. Transfer them to a large bowl, add the olive oil, and gently stir to coat.

Transfer the potatoes to the foil-lined baking sheet and arrange them in a single layer. Roast for 40 to 45 minutes, flipping them over in the pan halfway through the cooking time, until crispy and golden brown.

Transfer the potatoes to paper towels to drain off any excess oil. Toss the potatoes with the sauce and serve.

THE HOOK

⹀ FISH AND SEAFOOD MAIN COURSES ⹀

GRILLED LOBSTER TAIL, CIRCA 1995

This dish is one of the first things I saw that let me know I was in a different cooking world. I was working at what is now the Four Seasons Hotel in Atlanta (back then it was the Occidental Grand Hotel). There was a rooftop party and this was served. I had enjoyed butter-poached lobster when I worked at Salty's on Alki Beach in Seattle, but never a grilled lobster. You can do so much with this simple grilled lobster tail. You can cool it down and add it to a salad. You can add it to your favorite mac and cheese recipe, or to any other pasta dish. SERVES 4

Vegetable oil, for the grill

⅓ cup Smoked Paprika Compound Butter (page 49)

8 (4-ounce) lobster tails in the shell

1 teaspoon kosher salt

½ teaspoon freshly ground black pepper

3 tablespoons finely chopped fresh cilantro

Prepare a grill by setting up a two-zone cooking area. Arrange the coals so that you have a high-heat side and a medium-heat side where the coals are not as close to the grill grate. If you are using a gas grill, turn one burner to high, and the one next to it to medium.

Spray a thin coat of oil on the grill grates, or use a towel dipped in some oil to apply to the grates.

Place the compound butter in a small saucepan on the medium heat side of the grill, so it melts but doesn't burn.

Split and rinse the lobster tails with cold water and pat dry with paper towels. Place the tails meat-side down over the high heat side of the grill and cook for 4 minutes. Turn them over and then move them to the medium heat zone.

Baste the lobster with the melted butter. Then sprinkle with salt, pepper, and cilantro. Let the lobster poach in the butter that seeps into the lobster shell for 3 to 5 minutes on the grill. Cook until the internal temperature is to your preference. I prefer 120 degrees F, although the USDA says 145 degrees F.

I like to serve this up with something simple like grilled corn, with roasted potatoes, or with just some more butter and a beer.

CRAWFISH AND SHRIMP RISOTTO

The combination of crawfish and shrimp reminds me of my childhood in Louisiana—crawfish boils, hanging out at the park, listening to zydeco music. You'll love these flavors, too, whether you make it as a main dish or serve it as an appetizer. They are rooted in all our Southern sensibilities.

SERVES 4 AS AN ENTRÉE; 6 TO 8 AS AN APPETIZER

6 cups D's Chicken Stock
   (page 71) or store-bought

2 tablespoons extra-virgin olive oil

2 cups corn kernels from about
   3 ears, fresh or frozen

3 garlic cloves, sliced

1 medium yellow onion, diced

2 shallots, minced

1½ cups arborio rice

1 teaspoon kosher salt, plus
   more as needed

1 teaspoon freshly ground black
   pepper, plus more as needed

1 cup dry white wine

½ pound (21–25 per pound) shrimp,
   peeled, and deveined (you
   can use larger if you like)

½ pound Louisiana crawfish

2 ounces baby spinach,
   coarsely chopped

½ cup freshly grated Parmesan cheese

3 tablespoons butter

Zest of 1 lemon

In a large saucepan over high heat, bring the stock to a boil. Reduce the heat to low and keep warm.

In a large skillet or Dutch oven over medium heat, sauté the olive oil, corn, garlic, onion, shallots, rice, salt, and pepper for 5 minutes, until the onion is tender and the rice starts to smell toasty.

Add the wine and stir until the liquid is nearly absorbed by the rice. Add about 1 cup of the stock and stir until the stock is nearly absorbed before adding another ladleful. Cook, continuing to add stock, 1 cup at a time, for 20 to 30 minutes, until the rice is creamy and al dente. Be sure to taste the risotto when you're nearing the end of the stock. You may not need all the stock, or you may need more depending on the rice you use (check the package directions). Don't be afraid to add more stock if you need it.

Before all of the chicken stock is used, add the shrimp, crawfish, and spinach. Keep stirring for 5 to 7 minutes, until the shrimp are fully cooked.

Remove the pan from the heat and add the Parmesan cheese and butter. Season with more salt and pepper to taste, and the lemon zest. Transfer the risotto to a serving bowl or platter to pass around the table.

SAUTÉED ROYAL RED SHRIMP WITH BOURBON MAQUE CHOUX

This type of shrimp, called the Crown Jewel of Gulf Shrimp, comes from the deep waters (800 to 1,500 feet down) about 60 miles off the coast of Mexico. The season is late summer to late fall, with September being the best month. You can find them sold in coastal towns in the South or you can order them online. The average size is 16–20 to a pound, so they are large and taste like lobster and scallops. I have nothing against shrimp from other parts of the world, but the Royal Red Shrimp taste amazing! I pair them with Bourbon Maque Choux (page 117) because they are both sweet in their own different ways and complement each other. This dish is also colorful and easy to make—a real crowd-pleaser. SERVES 4

2 tablespoons extra-virgin olive oil

2 pounds Royal Red shrimp, or a local variety, peeled, and deveined (save the shells to make stock)

1 teaspoon kosher salt

½ teaspoon freshly ground black pepper

Bourbon Maque Choux (page 117)

Heat a large skillet over medium-high heat. Coat with the olive oil, and when you see the first hint of smoke, that's a sign the pan is hot enough.

Season the shrimp on both sides with the salt and pepper and then arrange them in the pan so there is some space between the shrimp. Cook for 2 minutes on each side. Set aside on a plate.

For an even more flavorful dish, use the same skillet to make the Bourbon Maque Choux. Just be sure to let the skillet cool for a minute or two after cooking the shrimp. When the Maque Choux is done, add the shrimp to bring up to temperature. Increase the heat to medium, for about 2 minutes (just long enough to get the shrimp hot) and serve.

FRIED OYSTERS AND CATFISH

To take my Uncle Bob's fish fry up a notch, I added curry powder and dill to this dish. Neither are a classic Southern thing, or even something my uncle would consider doing. Since I have been fortunate to work in a kitchen most of my life, I've been introduced to a lot of different cultures and developed an open mind and a willingness to try anything. SERVES 6 TO 8

2 cups buttermilk

3 tablespoons hot sauce of choice

1½ cups yellow cornmeal

½ cup all-purpose flour or gluten-free flour

1 tablespoon dried dill

1 teaspoon curry powder

2 teaspoons kosher salt

1 teaspoon freshly ground black pepper

1 tablespoon Creole seasoning

4 catfish fillets, cut in half

1 (1 pound) container gulf oysters, drained, and liquid discarded

3 cups vegetable oil, for frying

Whiskey Tartar Sauce (page 62)

Set a rack into a rimmed baking sheet. Layer a platter with paper towels.

In a shallow bowl, whisk together the buttermilk and hot sauce.

In a separate bowl, combine the cornmeal, flour, dill, curry powder, salt, pepper, and Creole seasoning and mix well.

Dip the catfish halves and oysters in the buttermilk mixture, then firmly press them into the cornmeal mixture, covering all sides completely and place them on the rack in the baking sheet. Cover and refrigerate for 15 to 20 minutes. This will help the cornmeal coating stick to the fish better during the frying process, and also give your frying oil time to heat up.

Heat the vegetable oil in a Dutch oven over medium heat until the oil shimmers. Using tongs, put the fish halves in the hot oil, a few at a time, swirling the fish a little in the hot oil before releasing it into the pan fully. This will help keep the fish from sinking to the bottom of the pot and sticking. Fry the fillets for 3 to 4 minutes on each side, until they are golden brown. Transfer the fish to the paper towel–lined platter. Then do the same with the oysters, frying them for only 2 to 3 minutes on each side. Transfer them to the platter with the fish.

Serve the oysters and catfish with the Whiskey Tartar Sauce alongside.

MUSSELS AND COLLARD GREENS WITH TOASTED BAGUETTE

This has become my signature dish, according to everyone who's tasted it. It was born in the Atlanta airport, traveled to Mobile, and now makes its way to your table. All you need is a Dutch oven, crusty bread, plates, spoons, and a shirt you don't mind getting a little mussel juice on. I like mussels as a finger food, but if you aren't so inclined, use a fork. SERVES 4 TO 6

COLLARD GREENS

2 tablespoons vegetable oil

4 slices bacon, cut in strips crosswise

2 shallots, julienned

3 garlic cloves, sliced

2 pounds (about 1 bunch) collard greens, stems removed, and julienned

4 bay leaves

1 tablespoon ground ginger

1 tablespoon minced fresh ginger

2 star anise pods

1 tablespoon coriander seed, crushed

1 teaspoon red pepper flakes

2½ cups D's Chicken Stock (page 71) or store-bought

¼ cup apple cider vinegar

MUSSELS

3 tablespoons vegetable oil

½ pound shiitake mushrooms, sliced

¼ cup julienned shallots

2 cup dry white wine

2½ pounds mussels, cleaned

2 teaspoons kosher salt

¾ cups D's Chicken Stock (page 71) or store-bought

2 tablespoons unsalted butter

1½ cups grape tomatoes, halved

2 tablespoons chopped fresh flat-leaf parsley

Toasted baguette slices, for serving

To make the collard greens, heat the oil in a large stockpot or Dutch oven over medium-high heat. Render the bacon until crispy. Add the shallots and garlic and sauté for 3 to 4 minutes, until translucent (not brown or burnt).

Reduce the heat to medium and add the greens, bay leaves, ground ginger, fresh ginger, star anise, coriander, and red pepper flakes. Stir to combine. Add the stock and vinegar, cover, and simmer for 40 minutes.

To make the mussels, heat the oil in a separate large stockpot or Dutch oven over medium heat. Add the mushrooms and cook for 2 to 3 minutes, until brown. Add the shallots and white wine and cook for 2 minutes. Add the mussels, salt, the cooked collard greens, and the stock and cook, stirring occasionally and watching the pot until all the mussels open and everything is cooked evenly. Discard any mussels that don't open. Add the butter, grape tomatoes, and parsley. Stir until the butter has melted, adjust the seasoning, and serve with some crusty bread.

CORNMEAL-DUSTED TROUT WITH GNOCCHI AND CARROT-CRAB LEMON CREAM SAUCE

I love to shallow fry fish because it's less messy and it's actually the best way to cook a thin fillet of fish. This gnocchi-veggie-fish casserole is the seafood version of chicken and dumplings, but way, way better. It's guaranteed to take top billing at your next shindig. Sometimes I call this a tart because the bed of gnocchi is similar to a dough crust, but with a savory topping. SERVES 4

CARROT-CRAB LEMON CREAM SAUCE

3 medium carrots, peeled and cut into ¼-inch-thick rounds

2 tablespoons extra-virgin olive oil

3 garlic cloves, sliced

2 shallots, julienned

½ cup Vegetable Stock (page 70) or store-bought

Juice of 1 lemon

Zest of 1 lemon, divided

1½ cups heavy cream

1 pound crab claw meat, shells removed

Potato Gnocchi (Potato Dumplings) (page 127)

1 bunch flat-leaf parsley, chopped

¼ teaspoon kosher salt

¼ teaspoon freshly ground black pepper

To make the cream sauce, bring a pot of water to a boil. Add the carrots and blanch for 3 to 5 minutes. Drain the carrots and set them aside in a bowl.

Heat the oil in a large skillet or Dutch oven over medium heat. Add the garlic and shallots and sauté for 3 to 5 minutes, until soft. Pour in the stock, increase the heat to medium-high, and bring to a gentle boil. Cook for 1 minute. Add the lemon juice and half the zest. Reduce the heat to medium, pour in the heavy cream, and bring to a gentle simmer. Add the crabmeat, gnocchi, and carrots. Cover, reduce the heat to medium-low, and simmer for 3 to 4 minutes.

Remove the lid. Give the mixture a good stir, then add the chopped parsley. Stir well, and cook, uncovered, for 3 to 4 minutes, until everything is hot. Season with salt and pepper.

CORNMEAL-DUSTED TROUT

1 cup cornmeal

2 teaspoons kosher salt

1 teaspoon freshly ground black pepper

1 teaspoon paprika

1 teaspoon cayenne pepper

4 (6-ounce) trout fillets, skin on

1 cup canola oil for frying, plus
    2 teaspoons to coat the fillets

To prepare the fish, in a medium bowl, combine the cornmeal, salt, pepper, paprika, and cayenne pepper. Mix well with a fork.

Coat the fish with 2 teaspoons of oil then dip each fillet in the cornmeal mixture, making sure to cover both sides.

Line a plate with paper towels. Heat the remaining 1 cup oil in a large cast-iron, or stainless-steel skillet over medium heat. Once the oil starts to shimmer, and working in batches, add the trout skin-side up to the pan. Cook for 3 minutes without moving the fish. Carefully flip the fish and cook another 3 minutes, until both sides are golden brown and crispy. Transfer the trout to the paper towel-lined plate to drain for a minute or two.

To serve, spoon the gnocchi and crab mixture onto four plates and place a trout fillet on top of each one.

SEARED REDFISH WITH FIELD PEAS, GREEN BEANS, SMOKED TURKEY, AND CHERRY-MISO SAUCE

I have cooked Sea Island red peas from South Carolina-based Anson Mills, and when I was in Mobile, Alabama, I used the ones from Dixie Lily, which were darker than the ones from Columbia. But the tastiest by far—and my favorite field pea for this recipe—is Lady Cream peas. With the power of the internet, you can find these dried beans online.

The fish and field peas pair well together because they are two complementary kinds of sweet. The fish gets its sweetness from what it eats, which is mostly shrimp. The peas get their sweetness from the soil and the sun. SERVES 4

FIELD PEAS, GREEN BEANS, AND SMOKED TURKEY

1 tablespoon butter

½ cup small dice onion

½ teaspoon red pepper flakes

3 garlic cloves, sliced

1 celery stalk, cut into small dice

½ cup small dice green bell pepper

1 tablespoon minced fresh ginger

2 bay leaves

3 cups dried field peas

4 cups D's Chicken Stock
(page 71), or Vegetable Stock
(page 70) or store-bought

½ pound smoked fresh turkey thighs,
pulled meat (see page 166)

1 teaspoon ground ginger

1½ teaspoons kosher salt

1 teaspoon freshly ground black pepper

1 cup green beans

To make the field peas, in a large heavy-bottom pot over medium-high heat, melt the butter and sauté the onion, red pepper flakes, garlic, celery, bell pepper, fresh ginger, and bay leaves for 2 minutes. Just as the onion and garlic start to brown, add the field peas, stock, smoked turkey, ground ginger, salt, and pepper and bring to a boil. Reduce the heat to low and simmer for 1 hour.

Add the green beans and continue to simmer for another 15 to 20 minutes, or until the peas and beans are tender. Check occasionally and add more water as needed to keep the peas covered–they like to be covered.

continued ➝

REDFISH

1 tablespoon extra-virgin olive oil

¾ teaspoon kosher salt

¼ teaspoon freshly ground
    black pepper

4 (6-ounce) red fish fillets, skinned

1 teaspoon Roasted Garlic-Herb
    Butter (page 50), thinly
    sliced for each fillet

Cherry-Miso Sauce (page 61)

To prepare the fish while the peas are cooking, heat the oil in a large cast-iron skillet over medium-high heat. (In my pan I've found it's best to sear 2 fillets at a time, so cook them in batches if your pan isn't that big.) Sprinkle salt and pepper over all the redfish.

Place the fillets skin-side down in hot oil, and cook 4 to 7 minutes undisturbed, until you see the fish start to brown along the bottom edges, and the flesh starts turning opaque about halfway up the side of the fillet, depending on the thickness of the fish.

Flip the fish over and remove the skillet from the heat. Allow the carry-over heat in the pan to continue to cook the fish. Add a slice of herb butter to each fillet and let it melt. By the time it melts, about 3 minutes, the fish is ready.

To serve, place the peas, beans, and turkey on serving plates, top with a piece of fish, and garnish with the Cherry-Miso Sauce.

GRILLED SNAPPER AND SHALLOTS WITH MUSTARD GREEN, LEEK, AND CREAM POTATO HASH

You can cook these fish either on a grill or in a cast-iron skillet. Make sure the skin is dry if you cook fish on a grill, otherwise it will stick to the grate. Always be sure the grill grate is clean and oil it by rubbing it with a folded paper towel dipped in olive oil. SERVES 4

1 tablespoon kosher salt

2 teaspoons freshly ground black pepper

¼ teaspoon cayenne pepper

1 teaspoon ground coriander

2 teaspoons granulated onion

4 (6-ounce) red snapper fillets, skin on

2 tablespoons extra-virgin olive oil, divided, plus more for drizzling

8 small shallots, peeled, and cut in half

Juice of 1 lemon

Mustard Green, Leek, and Cream Potato Hash (page 123), prepared and kept warm

If you are using an outdoor gas grill, set it for medium-high, direct heat. Line a rimmed baking sheet with aluminum foil.

In a small bowl, combine the salt, pepper, cayenne pepper, coriander, and granulated onion and mix with a fork.

Pat the 4 fillets dry with paper towels, rub them with 1 tablespoon of oil, and season each fillet with the seasoning mix. Rub the shallots with the remaining 1 tablespoon oil.

Transfer the seasoned fish and oiled shallots to the prepared baking sheet. Place the fish on the grill grates, skin-side down, and the shallots cut-side down. Cover with the grill lid and cook for about 2 minutes, until the fillet bottoms turn opaque and a flat spatula can slide underneath the fish with little resistance. Flip the fish over, cover again, and grill 2 to 4 minutes longer, until the fish is almost completely opaque and the center of each fillet registers at least 130 degrees F.

The shallots should also be done at this time, if you are using small ones. (If you have larger shallots, they will take about 10 minutes to cook, so you may need to leave them a bit longer on the grill.)

Transfer the cooked fillets and shallots back to the baking sheet. Drizzle with olive oil and sprinkle lemon juice over the fish. Serve with the hash.

HEADLINERS

= MAIN COURSES =

ROASTED CARROTS AND GOLDEN BEET BABA GHANOUSH WITH PRESERVED LEMONS

I like to parboil the beets before roasting them to make them easy to peel, plus they can then be roasted together with the carrots and they will be done at the same time. This eggplant dish serves as a main entrée but it is also a great vegetarian appetizer. I like to serve it with naan, crackers, or various types of bread. SERVES 4 TO 6

CARROTS AND GOLDEN BEETS

2 teaspoons kosher salt, divided

½ pound (about 2 medium) golden beets

½ pound (about 3 medium) carrots, trimmed

2 tablespoons extra-virgin olive oil

1 tablespoon harissa spice

To make the carrots and beets, preheat the oven to 400 degrees F. Fill a large bowl with ice and water to create an ice bath.

Bring a medium pot of water seasoned with 1 teaspoon of salt to a simmer. Add the beets and cook 20 to 30 minutes, until fork tender. Drain the beets and plunge them into the ice bath to cool. Peel the beets and cut them into quarters. Cut the carrots into pieces roughly the same size as the beets.

Combine the beets and carrots on a roasting pan and toss with olive oil, the remaining 1 teaspoon salt, and the harissa spice. Roast for 30 minutes, or until the carrots are tender and slightly golden. Set aside.

continued ➛

BABA GHANOUSH

2 to 3 medium eggplants

4 tablespoons extra-virgin
   olive oil, divided

½ teaspoon kosher salt

½ teaspoon freshly ground
   black pepper

¼ cup lemon juice

3 tablespoons tahini paste

4 garlic cloves, shaved on a Microplane

3 tablespoons chopped fresh
   flat-leaf parsley

½ teaspoon ground cumin

½ teaspoon smoked paprika,
   plus more for garnish

¼ teaspoon cayenne pepper

1 tablespoon garam masala

1 tablespoon Quick Preserved
   Lemons (page 72), for garnish

Pomegranate arils (seeds), for garnish

Watermelon radish, thinly
   sliced, for garnish

To make the baba ghanoush, reduce the oven temperature to 375 degrees F.

Have a baking sheet close by. Trim off the top ends of the eggplants, then cut them in half horizontally. Drizzle the eggplant halves with 1 tablespoon olive oil and season with the salt and pepper. Place the eggplant halves flesh-side down on the baking sheet. Roast the eggplant for 30 to 40 minutes, or until it is soft to the touch. Set aside to cool.

When eggplant is cool enough to hold in your hand, scoop the flesh into a large strainer set over a bowl, and let the excess liquid drain out of the eggplant for 10 to 15 minutes. Discard the thick skin.

At this point, combine the lemon juice, the remaining 3 tablespoons olive oil, the tahini, and the strained eggplant in a food processor and process until smooth and creamy.

Scoop out the mixture into a large bowl, add the garlic shavings, parsley, cumin, smoked paprika, cayenne pepper, and garam masala and mix until everything is well incorporated.

To serve, spoon the baba ghanoush onto a platter. Surround the eggplant with the carrots and beets, sprinkle the preserved lemon over the top of the vegetables, and garnish with the pomegranate arils, smoked paprika, and sliced watermelon radish.

ZA'ATAR-SPICED BOK CHOY AND CURRY BLACK-EYED PEAS WITH CAULIFLOWER AND MUSHROOMS

If a variety show was a dish, this would be it—a mash-up of Middle Eastern spices, Thai green curry, Chinese cabbage, and Southern caviar—black-eyed peas. Like any good international agreement, they all well work together. The black-eyed peas need to be soaked overnight so be sure to start this recipe a day ahead of when you want to serve it. SERVES 6 TO 8

GRILLED BOK CHOY

2 bok choy, cut in quarters

1 tablespoon extra-virgin olive oil

¼ teaspoon kosher salt

¼ teaspoon freshly ground black pepper

1 teaspoon za'atar spice

To prepare the bok choy, brush the cut sides generously with olive oil. Sprinkle with salt and pepper.

Preheat a grill to medium-high. Place the bok choy on the grill grate, making sure they cannot drop below the grates. (Watch out for flare-ups from dripping oil.) Cover with the grill lid and cook for 3 to 4 minutes, until grill marks form. Flip them over, cover, and cook another 3 to 4 minutes, until the bok choy stems have softened. (If you don't have a grill, you can use an indoor grill pan over medium-high heat.)

When the bok choy is done, place them on a baking sheet, sprinkle with the za'atar spice, and set aside while you make the black-eyed peas.

continued ➛

CURRY BLACK-EYED PEAS

3 tablespoons extra-virgin olive oil

1 large yellow onion, coarsely chopped

4 garlic cloves, sliced

2 cups cremini mushrooms, cut in quarters

2 teaspoons kosher salt, divided

3 tablespoons curry powder

2 tablespoons green curry paste

3 cups dried black-eyed peas (soaked overnight)

1 (13.5-ounce) can unsweetened coconut milk

1½ cups cauliflower florets

1 teaspoon freshly ground black pepper

Juice of 1 lime

6 to 10 grape tomatoes, cut in half

¼ cup coarsely chopped cilantro, as garnish

To prepare the black-eyed peas, heat the oil in a large pot over medium-high heat. Add the onion, garlic, mushrooms, and a pinch of the salt and sauté for 5 to 7 minutes. Stir in the curry powder and curry paste and cook, stirring, until the onion and mushrooms are nicely coated with the spices.

Add the black-eyed peas and 3 cups water. Reduce the heat to medium-low, cover, and cook for about 20 minutes.

Stir in the coconut milk and the cauliflower florets, reduce the heat to low, and simmer, uncovered, for 20 to 30 minutes, or until the beans and cauliflower are tender.

Stir in the remaining salt, the pepper, and the lime juice. Taste and adjust the seasoning as necessary. Garnish with the chopped cilantro.

Serve this on a platter, with the black-eyed pea, cauliflower, and mushroom mixture on the bottom, the bok choy on top, and garnished with the grape tomato halves and cilantro.

TOASTED BARLEY AND BUTTERNUT SQUASH RISOTTO

This is no one-note dish. A risotto made with barley, in place of arborio rice. The toasted barley gives this vegetarian dish added depth and heartiness, which you wouldn't get otherwise. And the cranberries make it sing. SERVES 4 TO 6

RUM-SOAKED DRIED CRANBERRIES

1 cup dried cranberries

¾ cup rum

½ cup water

RISOTTO

1½ cups pearl barley

5½ cups Vegetable Stock (page 70), or store-bought

3 tablespoons extra-virgin olive oil

8 ounces cremini mushrooms, quartered

4 garlic cloves, sliced

1 medium onion, diced

1½ cups diced butternut squash

1 teaspoon kosher salt

1 teaspoon freshly ground black pepper

1 cup dry white wine

⅔ cup shaved Parmesan cheese, plus more as garnish

1½ tablespoons chopped fresh chives, plus more as garnish

To make the cranberries, place the cranberries in a clean mason jar. Pour the rum and water over the cranberries, stir to combine, seal the lid, and store in your fridge to soak for a minimum of 2 hours, or up to 3 days before using. The longer they sit, the better they taste.

To prepare the risotto, preheat the oven to 350 degrees F.

Toast the barley on a rimmed baking sheet for 8 to 10 minutes, until golden brown and fragrant. Set aside to cool.

In a medium saucepan over high heat, bring the stock to a boil. Reduce the heat to low, and simmer to keep warm.

Warm a large skillet or Dutch oven over medium-high heat. Once hot, add the olive oil and mushrooms and sauté for 1 minute to get a little color on them. Then add the garlic, onion, squash, salt, and pepper. Reduce the heat to medium and cook, stirring constantly, for 5 minutes. Stir in the toasted barley. Add the white wine and stir to deglaze the pan and cook, stirring occasionally, until the liquid is reduced by half.

Add 1 cup of the hot stock to the barley mixture and cook over medium heat, stirring frequently, until all the liquid is absorbed. Continue to add the stock, 1 cup at a time and stirring frequently, until the liquid is absorbed and the barley is al dente. This will take 30 to 40 minutes.

Stir in the Parmesan cheese and chives. Transfer the risotto to a serving dish and garnish with more Parmesan, chives, and Rum-Soaked Dried Cranberries.

LOADED SWEET POTATO

The fennel and red onion salad added to the sweet potatoes takes this recipe over the top. If you have leftover salad, try adding it to the Black-Eyed Pea Salad (page 103) for a fun flavor boost. If you have leftover lamb ragù, use it in the Lamb Burger Helper (page 182). SERVES 4

BAKED SWEET POTATO

4 medium-large sweet potatoes, scrubbed and patted dry

Curry Yogurt Sauce (page 63)

GROUND LAMB RAGÙ

2 tablespoons extra-virgin olive oil

1 pound ground lamb

½ yellow onion, cut into small dice

1 fennel bulb, tops trimmed (save to use in a salad)

4 garlic cloves, sliced

2 bay leaves

1¼ teaspoons kosher salt

¼ teaspoon freshly ground black pepper

2 teaspoons dried oregano

2 teaspoons cumin seeds

2 teaspoons ground coriander

2 teaspoons ground ginger

1 tablespoon smoked paprika

1 (28-ounce) can whole San Marzano tomatoes, puréed in a blender

1½ cups D's Chicken Stock (page 71) or store-bought

SHAVED FENNEL AND RED ONION SALAD

½ bulb fennel, thinly shaved

½ onion, thinly shaved

1 tablespoon chopped parsley

2 tablespoons extra-virgin olive oil

¼ teaspoon kosher salt

¼ teaspoon freshly ground black pepper

To make the potatoes, preheat the oven to 400 degrees F. Line a rimmed baking sheet with parchment paper.

Poke a few holes all over the potatoes with a fork to release steam while baking. Place the potatoes on the prepared baking sheet, leaving some space between each, and bake for 45 minutes, or until they are easily pierced with a knife. Let them cool for 5 minutes before cutting open lengthwise.

To make the lamb ragù, heat the oil in a large heavy-bottom pot or Dutch oven over medium-high heat. Add the ground lamb and cook for 5 to 7 minutes, breaking it up as it cooks, until browned. Turn the heat off and use a ladle to discard about half of the fat.

Turn the heat back on to medium-high, and add the onion, fennel, garlic, bay leaves, salt, pepper, oregano, cumin seeds, coriander, ginger, and smoked paprika. Cook for 10 minutes, stirring occasionally, until the fennel and onion are tender.

Add the puréed tomatoes and stock, and stir until well combined. Reduce the heat to low, cover, and simmer for 20 to 30 minutes.

To make the fennel salad, in a medium bowl, combine the fennel, onion, parsley, and olive oil. Give it a quick toss, add the salt and pepper, and toss again to coat everything.

To assemble the dish, place some yogurt sauce on the bottom of each plate, add a potato, top with a portion of the lamb ragù, and then a final topping of ¼ of the salad. If any sauce is left over, pass it around the table for anyone who might like a bit more.

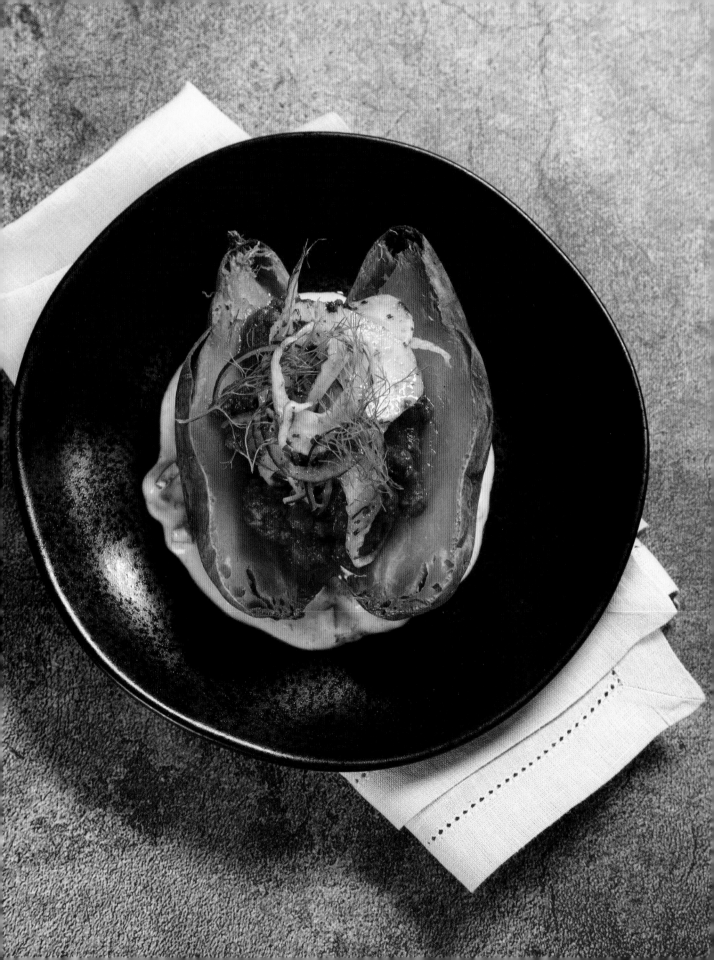

DUCK SANDWICH WITH PEANUT-FIG RELISH AND BOURBON RAISIN SLAW

This sandwich became a hit at One Flew South with both the airport staff and travelers. My thought process for this was to make a sandwich with pulled duck instead of using the more traditional Southern pulled barbecue pork. This sandwich has a dedicated following, which is why it made its way into this book. If you already have the various elements already made and stored in your pantry, it should be a breeze to throw together. Pair it with tater tots and don't apologize to anyone! MAKES 4 SANDWICHES

12 ounces Duck Confit (see Duck Confit Hash, page 124) pulled into pieces

1 tablespoon pickled ginger, available at most grocery stores

1/2 cup D's Chicken Stock (page 71) or store-bought

Scant 1/2 cup Jazzed-Up Hoisin Sauce (page 55)

2 teaspoons lemon juice

4 brioche buns

1 1/2 tablespoons butter

1/2 cup Curry-Mustard Spread (page 53)

4 tablespoons Peanut-Fig Relish (page 68)

1 1/2 cups Bourbon-Raisin Slaw (page 100)

In a medium saucepan over medium heat, combine the pulled duck, pickled ginger, stock, hoisin sauce, and lemon juice and stir. When the mixture is hot, set aside.

Melt the butter in a cast-iron skillet or pan over medium heat, using a spatula to swirl it around to coat the pan. Place the buns cut-side down onto the skillet and cook for 30 to 40 seconds, or until golden brown and toasted. You may need to do this in batches. Watch closely so you don't go past golden brown.

To build the sandwich, spread the Curry-Mustard Spread on the top bun, spread a little fig relish on the bottom bun, and the place duck confit on top of the fig relish. Add the slaw and finish with the top bun and enjoy.

Note: The Curry-Mustard Spread is made with mayonnaise and gets its yellow color from the curry.

KENTUCKYAKI DRUMSTICKS

Here is my recipe for the most deliciously simple baked drumsticks, which are then slathered with my favorite Kentuckyaki Sauce, which you can find online at bourbonbarrelfoods.com. Serve these with the Dirty Rice (page 170). SERVES 4

2 tablespoons extra-virgin olive oil

8 chicken drumsticks, rinsed and patted dry

¼ cup reduced sodium soy sauce

1 teaspoon granulated garlic

1 teaspoon granulated onion

¼ teaspoon kosher salt

¼ teaspoon freshly ground black pepper

1½ cups Kentuckyaki Sauce

1 teaspoon cornstarch

1 tablespoon chopped fresh cilantro, for garnish, optional

Sliced green onions, for garnish

Sesame seeds, for garnish

Preheat the oven to 400 degrees F. Line a baking sheet with aluminum foil.

In a large bowl combine the oil, soy sauce, garlic, onion, salt, and pepper and mix well. Add the drumsticks and toss until they are fully coated in the mixture.

Arrange the drumsticks on the prepared baking sheet and bake for 25 to 30 minutes, flipping the drumsticks halfway through the cooking time.

Heat the Kentuckyaki Sauce in a saucepan over medium-high heat. In a small bowl, make a slurry by whisking together the cornstarch and 2 teaspoons water until all lumps are gone.

When the Kentuckyaki Sauce starts to boil, add the slurry and stir until the sauce thickens. Set aside to cool.

Transfer the cooked chicken to a serving platter and drizzle the sauce over the legs. Garnish with the chopped cilantro, if using, green onions, and sesame seeds and serve.

BERBERE-SPICED FRIED CHICKEN THIGHS

You can find Berbere spice at most ethnic or high-end grocery stores, or you can order online. Berbere is a warm spice, adding a tiny amount of heat. In West Africa, this is a basic spice similar to the Indian culture's garam masala. Serve with the Coconut Cream Corn and Potatoes (page 126).

SERVES 4 TO 6

CHICKEN MARINADE

5 cups vegetable oil, divided

3 green onions, cut in half

3 garlic cloves

1 jalapeño, sliced and seeds removed

2 teaspoons ground ginger

1 tablespoon Berbere spice, plus more for serving

¼ teaspoon ground cloves

1 ounce Worcestershire sauce

2 teaspoons kosher salt, plus more for serving

2 teaspoons freshly ground black pepper

8 boneless skinless chicken thighs, excess fat removed

Coconut Cream Corn and Potatoes (page 126), for serving

SEASONED FLOUR

2 cups potato starch

2 cups cornstarch

¼ cup Berbere spice

1 tablespoon kosher salt

To make the marinade, in a blender, add 1½ to 2 cups of the oil, green onions, garlic, jalapeño, ginger, Berbere spice, ground cloves, Worcestershire sauce, salt, and pepper. Blend until smooth.

Place the chicken thighs in a nonreactive container and add the marinade. Cover, and refrigerate for at least 4 hours, or overnight for the best flavor.

To make the seasoned flour, place potato starch, cornstarch, Berbere spice, and salt in a large bowl and mix well with a wire whisk.

Line a baking sheet with parchment paper.

Remove 1 piece of chicken at a time from the marinade and dredge in the seasoned flour mixture until thoroughly coated on all sides. Place the fully coated chicken onto the prepared baking sheet and let sit for 10 to 15 minutes.

While the chicken is resting, heat 3 cups of oil in a Dutch oven on high heat until it reaches 350 degrees F. Fry each piece of chicken for 6 to 7 minutes, turning after 3 minutes to insure it evenly browns on all sides. The internal temperature of the chicken should read 165 degrees F on a meat thermometer.

Place the chicken pieces on a wire rack or paper towels, to drain some of the oil away. Season with additional Berbere spice and a pinch of salt.

When you are ready to serve, arrange the chicken pieces atop a bed of the Coconut Cream Corn and Potatoes. Enjoy!

BERBERE-SPICED FRIED CHICKEN SANDWICH

You can use the same method of cooking the chicken thighs that is used in the Berbere-Spiced Fried Chicken Thighs (page 163) to make these lunch or game day sandwiches. Just be sure to buy the boneless thighs. SERVES 4

CHICKEN MARINADE

1 cup buttermilk

1 teaspoon Berbere spice

1/2 teaspoon garlic powder

1/2 teaspoon onion powder

1 teaspoon kosher salt

4 boneless skinless chicken thighs, rinsed and patted dry, extra fat removed

BREADING

1 cup cornstarch

1 cup potato starch

1 teaspoon kosher salt

1/2 teaspoon garlic powder

1/2 teaspoon onion powder

1/4 teaspoon freshly ground black pepper

SANDWICHES

3 cups vegetable oil, for frying

2 teaspoons Berbere spice

1/8 teaspoon kosher salt

4 burger buns, toasted

1 cup Bourbon-Raisin Slaw (page 100)

1/2 cup Pickled Fresno Peppers and Shallots (page 77)

BERBERE-SPICED MAYO

1/2 cup Roasted Garlic Aioli (page 52)

2 teaspoons Berbere spice

To make the marinade, combine the buttermilk, Berbere spice, garlic powder, onion powder, and salt in a medium mixing bowl. Add the chicken thighs and use tongs to ensure they are evenly coated.

Cover the bowl with plastic wrap and marinate in the refrigerator at least 4 hours or up to overnight. Remove the chicken from the fridge 20 to 30 minutes before cooking, to bring it to room temperature.

To make the breading, combine the cornstarch, potato starch, salt, garlic powder, onion powder, and pepper in a shallow dish and mix well with a fork.

To prepare the chicken, dredge each of the chicken thighs in the breading mixture, making sure to completely coat each thigh and set aside on a platter.

Line baking sheet with paper towels and set a wire rack on top. Heat the oil in a large heavy bottom pot, or Dutch oven and heat to 350 degrees F. Place a chicken thigh in the hot oil and fry for 4 to 6 minutes on each side, until it's a deep golden brown and has a crunchy texture. The internal temperature of the chicken should read 165 degrees F on a meat thermometer. Transfer the thigh to the wire rack to drain on the paper towels underneath.

Bring the heat back up to 350 degrees F and repeat the process with the rest of the chicken thighs. Season the fried chicken thighs with the Berbere spice and salt.

To prepare the mayo, combine the garlic aioli and Berbere spice in a small bowl.

To assemble the sandwiches, spoon 2 teaspoons of the mayo on each toasted bun. Then layer the slaw on each of the bottom buns and top with a piece of the chicken. Add some of the pickled peppers and shallots and top with the remaining buns.

SMOKED CHICKEN AND BACON FETTUCCINE

This is a quick one-pot dish when you have all your ingredients ready to go. The first time I made this, it was basically a clean-out-the-fridge dinner. I was watching some game on TV at my business partner's house and saw that he had some leftover smoked chicken. It was my turn to provide the food, and I hadn't brought anything. So, I threw this pasta dish together using ingredients from his kitchen. If you don't own your own smoker, buy a smoked chicken at your local barbecue joint. SERVES 8 TO 10

SMOKED CHICKEN

1 gallon Citrus Brine (page 69)

2 whole chickens, each split in half

3 tablespoons vegetable oil

3 tablespoons Basic SoNat Rub (page 44)

TOASTED PECANS

½ cup pecan pieces

1 tablespoon extra-virgin olive oil

½ teaspoon kosher salt

To prepare the chicken, Pour the Citrus Brine into a very large container with a lid and add the chickens. Seal with the lid and refrigerate for at least 4 hours, or up to overnight.

Set up your smoker for dual-zone smoking: direct and indirect heat. Preheat the smoker to 225 degrees F. Place the grate level high and in the indirect heat zone. I like to smoke with pecan wood, but you can use whatever you like. While that's getting up to temperature, continue to work on the chicken.

Pat the brined chicken dry with paper towels. Rub the chickens all over with oil. Sprinkle the SoNat Rub evenly on all sides of the chicken halves, patting it down to make the seasoning stick. Set aside on a platter and let come to room temperature before it goes on the grill.

Transfer the chicken to the grate in the smoker, skin-side up, and smoke over indirect heat for 1½ to 2 hours, or until the internal temperature for the breast is about 160 degrees F, and the leg and thigh are about 180 degrees F. Transfer the chicken to a platter and let it cool to room temperature.

When cool enough to handle, pull the chicken meat from the bone and set aside until ready to use in the pasta dish.

To prepare the pecans, preheat the oven to 350 degrees F. Line a rimmed baking sheet with aluminum foil.

In a small bowl toss the pecans in the oil and salt. Arrange the pecans in a single layer on the baking sheet and bake for 7 to 10 minutes, stirring occasionally, until they are browned and fragrant. Let cool.

BACON FETTUCCINE

1 (16-ounce) package fettuccine, or your favorite variety

2 slices bacon

2 shallots, julienned

1½ cups D's Chicken Stock (page 71) or store-bought

1½ cups heavy cream

1 tablespoon Dijon mustard

Juice of 1 lemon

4 cups baby arugula

2 teaspoons kosher salt

1 teaspoon freshly ground black pepper

1 cup fresh or frozen peas

1 pound smoked chicken, pulled meat

½ cup freshly grated Parmesan cheese, for garnish

To prepare the fettuccine, bring a large pot of salted water to boil. Add the fettuccine and cook until al dente, according to the package directions. Drain and set aside.

In a small skillet, cook the bacon slices until crispy. Reserve the fat. Crumble the crispy bacon to use for the topping; set aside.

Heat 1 tablespoon of the reserved bacon fat in a Dutch oven over medium-high heat. Add the shallots and sauté for 1 minute, until they are soft. Reduce the heat, add the stock and heavy cream, and simmer for 5 minutes, until the cream mixture slightly thickens.

Stir in the mustard, lemon juice, arugula, salt, pepper, peas, cooked pasta, and the pulled chicken into the Dutch oven and mix well. Cook for 3 minutes to let the sauce thicken and for everything to warm up and get to know each other.

Garnish with the Parmesan cheese, the bacon crumbles, and 2 tablespoons toasted pecans (you will have leftover pecans for another use).

....

Notes: You can use the smoked chicken with other sides you love and it will be good in all kinds of things—chicken salad or smoked chicken tacos are a couple suggestions. It's all up to your imagination. This recipe for smoked chicken also works well with turkey thighs. Try it in the Seared Redfish with Field Peas, Green Beans, Smoked Turkey, and Cherry-Miso Sauce (page 142).

FRIED CHICKEN LIVERS WITH BRUSSELS SPROUTS KIMCHI AND SRIRACHA MAYO

The Brussels Sprouts Kimchi adds a spicy crunch to the sweetness of the livers. This is an easy but impressive main course to pass around the table. SERVES 6 TO 8

BRUSSELS SPROUTS KIMCHI

½ cup thinly sliced Brussels sprouts

1 cup kimchi, of choice

SRIRACHA MAYO

1 cup mayonnaise

2 tablespoons sriracha

Juice of 1 lime

FRIED CHICKEN LIVERS

1 cup buttermilk

¼ cup hot sauce (I prefer Crystal Hot Sauce)

1 tablespoon fish sauce

2 tablespoons soy sauce

1 pound chicken livers, trimmed and rinsed

1 cup all-purpose flour

½ cup cornmeal

2 teaspoons cayenne pepper

2 teaspoons freshly ground black pepper

1 teaspoon kosher salt

2 teaspoons garlic powder

1 teaspoon onion powder

¼ teaspoon paprika

4 cups vegetable oil, for frying

To make the kimchi, combine the Brussels sprouts and kimchi in a medium bowl, mix well, and set aside until ready to use.

To make the mayo, in a small bowl, mix together the mayonnaise, sriracha, and lime juice, cover, and refrigerate until ready to use.

To make the chicken livers, combine the buttermilk, hot sauce, fish sauce, and soy sauce in a large bowl and stir well to make the marinade. Place the livers in the buttermilk mixture to soak for at least 30 minutes. They do not need to be refrigerated.

In a shallow dish, whisk together the flour, cornmeal, cayenne pepper, pepper, salt, garlic powder, onion powder, and paprika.

Fit a wire rack into a rimmed baking sheet. Heat the oil in a Dutch oven, or fryer over medium heat and bring the temperature to 350 degrees F.

Remove the chicken livers from the marinade and dredge each one in the dry mixture, making sure to coat all sides and place them on a plate or second baking sheet. Working in batches, add the livers to the hot oil and fry for 2 minutes on each side.

Transfer the fried livers to the wire rack to drain.

Serve the fried chicken livers on a platter. Sprinkle the Brussels Sprouts Kimchi over the livers and top with dollops of the Sriracha Mayo.

DIRTY RICE

This is one of the old Louisiana dishes I grew up eating around holiday time. It's a good way to use up organ meats left over from other dishes. It makes a great side dish with a holiday ham or turkey—plus, it only takes about 30 minutes to prepare. I like to use Kentuckyaki Sauce (you can buy it online) in this rice, a sweet-savory sauce made with soy sauce, sorghum, and bourbon that you can order online at bourbonbarrelfoods.com. SERVES ABOUT 8

2 tablespoons vegetable oil

½ pound ground bulk sausage (my mom always used chicken gizzards—try it!)

½ pound chicken livers

1 medium yellow onion, diced

1 green bell pepper, seeded, and diced

½ cup diced celery

5 garlic cloves, sliced

3 teaspoons Creole seasoning

2 cups long-grain rice, rinsed (basmati is good, too)

4 cups D's Chicken Stock (page 71) or store-bought

1 tablespoon Kentuckyaki Sauce

3 bay leaves

2 teaspoons dry thyme

Kosher salt

Freshly ground black pepper

¼ cup chopped fresh flat-leaf parsley, for garnish

¼ cup sliced green onions, for garnish

Heat the oil in a heavy-bottom saucepan or Dutch oven over medium-high heat. Add the ground sausage and chicken livers and cook, stirring often, until the meat is no longer pink.

Add the onion, bell pepper, celery, and garlic and cook for 3 to 4 minutes until the onion has softened.

Add the Creole seasoning, rice, stock, Kentuckyaki Sauce, bay leaves, and thyme, and season with salt and pepper to taste. Stir, increase the heat to high, and bring to a boil. Reduce the heat to low, cover, and simmer for 20 to 25 minutes, or until the rice is cooked and the liquid has been absorbed. Remove from the heat and allow to rest for about 5 minutes.

Fluff with a fork and garnish with parsley and green onions.

BARBECUE PORK PIZZA

No joke, you read that title correctly. After a catering event at our Mobile restaurant, I had some leftover pork. I have a small obsession with pizza and I love anything smoked, so I couldn't think of anything better to do with leftover smoked pork than put it on a pizza.

You can use your favorite barbecue pork recipe or go to your favorite barbecue joint and pick up some smoked pork. Plan ahead if you make your own dough from the provided recipe. It needs to be made a day ahead of when you want to use it. MAKES 1 (10-INCH) PIZZA

½ cup sliced baby portabello mushrooms

2 tablespoons vegetable oil

1 pizza dough ball (page 172)

⅓ cup Pizza Sauce (page 64)

1 cup pulled pork, left over or store-bought

¾ cup shredded low-moisture mozzarella cheese

½ cup sliced red onion

2 tablespoons Balsamic Barbecue Sauce (page 58) or sauce of choice

¼ cup chopped cilantro

1 tablespoon sliced green onion

Place a pizza baking steel or stone in the oven and preheat to 500 degrees F. Heat for at least 30 minutes before using.

In a small skillet, sauté the mushrooms in the oil until softened.

On a lightly floured surface, roll the pizza dough out into a 10-inch circle. Place on a pizza peel that has been covered with parchment paper. If you don't have a pizza peel, or an instrument to use to transfer the pizza to the over, use the bottom side of a baking sheet.

Evenly spread the Pizza Sauce over the dough. Add the pulled pork, mushrooms, mozzarella cheese, and red onion. Place the pizza in the preheated oven. If using a stone, place the sheet pan next to your stone, and pull the parchment paper with the pizza onto the stone. Bake for 10 to 12 minutes, until the crust is a golden brown.

Remove from oven and cool for a few minutes. Then garnish with a swirl of the barbecue sauce and a sprinkling of cilantro and green onion.

continued ·➤

PIZZA DOUGH

I like to make this a day before I use it; the longer, slower rise in the dough gives the gluten time to relax and strengthen, allowing for better flavor and elasticity.

Bakingsteel.com is a great resource for starting your pizza nerd journey. They have equipment, recipes, and even classes. MAKES DOUGH FOR 2 (10-INCH) PIZZAS

2¼ teaspoons active dry yeast

1 tablespoon honey

2¾ cups 00 flour (I use King Arthur 00 flour)

2 tablespoons extra-virgin olive oil

1 teaspoon kosher salt

In the bowl of a stand mixer, combine 1 cup warm water, the yeast, and honey. Set aside for 5 to 10 minutes to allow the yeast to become active and foamy. (If you are not seeing any activity after 10 minutes, start over with a fresh yeast.)

Add the flour, olive oil, and salt. Using a dough hook, knead the dough on medium speed for 6 minutes, or until it is soft and smooth and pulls cleanly away from the sides of the bowl.

Shape the dough into a ball, place it in a large, lightly oiled bowl, and cover the bowl tightly with plastic wrap. Place in a warm spot to rise for 20 to 30 minutes or until the dough has doubled in size.

Lightly punch down the dough then transfer to a lightly floured work surface. Divide the dough into 2 balls.

Lightly flour a storage container for the 2 balls. If you want to use the dough the same day, after you cut the dough into 2 balls, cover, and let rise again for about 30 minutes.

If you are baking the next day, cover tightly, and refrigerate overnight, or up to 3 days. Remove from the fridge and set aside 1½ hours before using, or until the dough comes to room temperature.

COFFEE-RUBBED GRILLED PORK TENDERLOIN WITH RED-EYE GRAVY

The tenderloin is the most tender piece of meat on most animals because of where it is located. It doesn't do anything except taste really good—as the name hints. Because of its mild flavor, it can take bold flavors and not get lost in them. I like to use a Heritage pork such as Duroc or Berkshire when I can. This dish pairs really well with the Mustard Green, Leek, and Cream Potato Hash (page 123) or the Yellow Rice and Bok Choy Hoppin' John (page 121). SERVES 4

2 tablespoons Coffee Rub (page 45)

2 pounds pork tenderloin, trimmed and silver skin removed

2 tablespoons extra-virgin olive oil

SoNat Red-Eye Gravy (page 65)

Preheat the oven 350 degrees F. Rub the pork all over with the coffee rub and let sit for 20 minutes.

Heat the oil in a medium oven-safe skillet over medium-high heat. Add the pork and cook for 4 minutes, turning frequently so the spices don't burn and become bitter, until brown on all sides.

Transfer the skillet to the oven and bake for 15 minutes, rotating the pan after 7 minutes. The tenderloin is done when the internal temperature of the meat reads 155-160 degrees F (it will be slightly pink). Transfer the tenderloin to a cutting board and let rest at room temperature for 10 minutes. Cut the pork crosswise into ½-inch-thick slices.

If the Red-Eye Gravy is not already made, make it in the same skillet once it is cool enough to handle.

ASIAN MEATLOAF

Meatloaf was one of my all-time favorites when I was growing up, and when you're a chef, you start to play with the flavors you grew up with. My mom's meatloaf was big on my hit list, but I wanted to look at the recipe through a new lens. I removed the ketchup and added hoisin sauce and lots of ginger and green onion, coriander, and star anise. Then I made a balsamic barbecue sauce to accompany it. Guaranteed yum! SERVES 6 TO 8

MEATLOAF SEASONING

1 tablespoon coriander seeds

½ cup black peppercorns

5 star anise pods

MEATLOAF

2 pounds lean ground beef

6 green onions, finely chopped

2 garlic cloves, grated

½ teaspoon grated fresh ginger

1 shallot, finely chopped

2 tablespoons finely chopped fresh chives

2 tablespoons Jazzed-Up Hoisin Sauce (page 55)

2 eggs, beaten

1 cup plain panko breadcrumbs

2 teaspoons kosher salt

2 tablespoons canola oil

1 tablespoon Meatloaf Seasoning

Balsamic Barbecue Sauce (page 58)

To make the meatloaf seasoning, combine the coriander seeds, peppercorns, and star anise in a sauté pan over high heat and cook, stirring often, until they are warmed through, toasted, and fragrant.

Transfer the spices to a bowl to cool for 5 minutes. Transfer the spice mixture to an electric spice grinder and grind them to a fine powder. Shake them through a fine-mesh strainer into a bowl to remove any larger pieces. The spice mixture can be stored in an airtight container in your spice cabinet for up to 6 months, as you won't need it all for this recipe.

To make the meatloaf, preheat the oven to 400 degrees F.

In a large bowl, combine the ground beef, green onions, garlic, ginger, shallot, chives, hoisin sauce, eggs, panko, salt, canola oil, and 1 tablespoon Meatloaf Seasoning and mix just until well combined. Do not overmix the meatloaf or it will become tough when cooked.

Spray an 8-inch loaf pan with nonstick cooking spray and press the meatloaf mixture in to form a loaf. Cook for 1 hour, or until golden brown and fully cooked through.

Serve with Balsamic Barbecue Sauce.

Notes: Try adding a dollop of Pimento Cheese (page 82) to slices of meatloaf on Texas toast for a great open-faced sandwich.

I try to purchase my beef from a local source, and prefer grass-fed.

FENNEL-BRAISED SHORT RIBS

This dish is a good example of tasting and understanding the nuances in cooking. For example, I do not like the taste of black licorice, but I love fennel and fennel seeds and star anise. On paper this probably doesn't make any sense, but when you taste these braised short ribs, they blend with all the other flavors in the pot and the ribs melt in your mouth.

This recipe requires seasoning the short ribs the day before you cook. Short ribs are a fatty meat and there will be a good deal of fat in the sauce. Simply strain it through a 4-cup fat separator (a measuring cup with a spout at the bottom, available online). Serve the short ribs with the Pickled Carrots (page 74), which will cut through the richness of this dish. SERVES 4 TO 6

DRY RUB SEASONING

3 tablespoons Chinese five-spice powder

2 tablespoons garlic powder

2 tablespoons freshly ground black pepper

½ cup ground fennel seeds

3 tablespoons ground coriander

2 tablespoons red pepper flakes

1 cup brown sugar

To make the dry rub, in a medium mixing bowl, combine the five-spice powder, garlic powder, pepper, fennel, coriander, red pepper flakes, and brown sugar. Reserve ¼ cup of dry rub seasoning and store the remaining seasoning in an airtight container for future use.

SHORT RIBS

8 bone-in short ribs (about 4 pounds total), trimmed of excess fat

4 tablespoons canola oil, divided

½ large sweet onion, diced

1 fennel bulb, diced, and fronds, stems, and core discarded

1 tablespoon grated fresh ginger

2 carrots, diced

1 tablespoon kosher salt

2 teaspoons freshly ground black pepper

1 cup red wine

1 cup orange juice

2 cups beef stock

2 cups D's Chicken Stock (page 71) or store-bought

Cooked rice or mashed potatoes, for serving

To make the ribs, coat the ribs with 1 tablespoon canola oil. Rub the ribs all over with the reserved ¼ cup of dry rub seasoning and place them in a bowl. Cover the ribs with plastic wrap and place them in the refrigerator to marinate for at least 1 hour or up to 24 hours.

When you are ready to cook the ribs, preheat the oven to 350 degrees F.

Using a paper towel, pat the ribs dry, but don't rub off the spices. Heat 1 tablespoon canola oil in a large, oven-safe pan over medium heat, and brown the meat for 3 minutes on each side. Transfer the meat to a baking sheet and set aside. Discard most of the remaining fat in the pan.

Add the remaining 2 tablespoons canola oil to the pan and return to medium heat. Add the onion, fennel, ginger, carrots, salt, and pepper. Cook for 8 minutes, stirring occasionally, until the vegetables have softened and the onion is lightly browned.

Add the red wine to deglaze the pan and cook for about 5 minutes to reduce the liquid by half. Add the orange juice and stocks, and increase the heat to bring the mixture to a boil. Return the ribs to the pan, cover with a lid, and transfer to the oven. Bake for 4 hours, or until fork tender.

Before you serve, remove the bones from the pan and discard. Spoon the rice or potatoes into individual serving bowls and top with the meat and sauce.

CAST-IRON SEARED NEW YORK STRIP WITH MOJO POTATOES AND MUSTARD GREEN CHIMICHURRI

Make sure your pan is ripping hot when you add the steak to the pan. A quick sear seals in the flavor. Serving the steak with the potatoes and chimichurri takes it to a new level! SERVES 2

1 (12-ounce) New York strip steak

1 teaspoon kosher salt

½ teaspoon freshly ground black pepper

1 tablespoon extra-virgin olive oil

1 tablespoon butter

4 sprigs thyme

1 clove garlic, crushed

Mojo Potatoes (page 128), for serving

Mustard Green Chimichurri (page 54), for serving

Let the steak come up to room temperature for 30 to 40 minutes before cooking.

When you are ready to cook, sprinkle the salt and pepper evenly over the steak. Heat the oil in a large cast-iron skillet over high heat and swirl to coat. Cook the steak for 3 to 4 minutes on each side, or until browned.

Reduce the heat to medium-low and add the butter, thyme, and garlic to the pan. Using an oven mitt or folded dish towel to tilt the pan toward you so the butter pools, continue to cook for 1½ minutes, basting the steak with butter continuously with a spoon and turning the steak over a few times to ensure even cooking, until you reach your desired degree of doneness. Transfer the steak to a platter and set aside at room temperature for 10 minutes.

To serve, slice the steak and arrange on the plate with the potatoes on the side, and the chimichurri sauce in the middle for dipping.

LAMB BURGER HELPER

Trying to recapture my childhood favorites when I was creating the menu for Southern National, I came up with this little piece of nostalgia—a guaranteed parent and child-pleaser! Serve with Kool-Aid and 2 cubes of ice. SERVES 8

1 (28-ounce) can whole San Marzano tomatoes

1 tablespoon plus 1¼ teaspoons kosher salt, divided

1 pound mini rigatoni

2 tablespoons extra-virgin olive oil

1 pound ground lamb

½ yellow onion, cut into small dice

1 fennel bulb, tops trimmed (save to use in a salad), and diced

4 garlic cloves, sliced

2 bay leaves

¼ teaspoon freshly ground black pepper

2 teaspoons dried oregano

2 teaspoons cumin seeds

2 teaspoons ground coriander

2 teaspoons ground ginger

1 tablespoon smoked paprika

1 teaspoon red pepper flakes

1½ cups D's Chicken Stock (page 71) or store-bought

½ cup shredded Parmesan cheese

1½ cups shredded mozzarella cheese

½ bunch fresh flat-leaf parsley, chopped

Preheat the oven 350 degrees F. Spray or oil a 9 x 13-inch casserole dish and set aside.

Purée the tomatoes in a blender on medium speed and set aside.

Bring a large pot of water with 1 tablespoon salt to a boil over high heat. Add the pasta and cook, stirring occasionally, according to the package directions for al dente. Drain the pasta in a colander and transfer to a large bowl.

Heat the oil in a large heavy-bottom pot or Dutch oven over medium-high heat. Add the ground lamb and cook for 5 to 7 minutes, breaking it up it up as it cooks, until browned. Turn the heat off and use a ladle to discard about half of the fat.

Turn the heat back on to medium-high and add the onion, fennel, garlic, bay leaves, 1¼ teaspoons salt, pepper, oregano, cumin seeds, coriander, ginger, smoked paprika, and red pepper flakes. Cook for 10 minutes, stirring occasionally, until the fennel and onion are tender.

Add the puréed tomatoes and stock and stir until well combined. Reduce the heat to low, cover, and simmer for 20 to 30 minutes.

Remove the bay leaves from the sauce and pour the sauce over the pasta. Add the Parmesan cheese and toss with a large spoon until well combined. Transfer the pasta mixture to the casserole dish and top with the mozzarella cheese. Cover the dish with aluminum foil and bake for 20 minutes, until the sauce is bubbly around the edges of the casserole.

Remove the foil and bake another 10 minutes, until the cheese is melted and starting to brown. Garnish with chopped parsley.

Note: A tasty variation is to stir 3 cups of fresh spinach and arugula into the finished sauce before tossing over the pasta.

CURTAIN · CALLS

⹀ DESSERT ⹀

BOURBON AND ORANGE MIXED BERRIES

These berries are great as a dessert with whipped cream, or alone, as a lovely addition to your morning yogurt. Use them on Citrus Pound Cake with Buttermilk and Bourbon (page 198).

MAKES 3 CUPS

1 cup strawberries, tops removed and quartered

¾ cup raspberries, halved

¾ cup blueberries

¾ cup blackberries, halved

2 tablespoons sugar

2 tablespoons bourbon

Zest and juice of 1 orange

Whipped Cream (see below), optional

Place the strawberries, raspberries, blueberries, and blackberries in a medium bowl. Add the sugar, bourbon, zest, and orange juice. Stir well to coat all the berries.

Cover and refrigerate for at least 1 hour to allow all the flavors to combine. The berries will begin to soften and release some of their liquid during this time, and they will become more delicious the longer they sit.

WHIPPED CREAM

MAKES APPROXIMATELY 2 CUPS

1 cup heavy whipping cream

2 tablespoons powdered sugar

½ teaspoon vanilla extract

Place the bowl of a stand mixer along with the whisk in the freezer for 10 to 15 minutes to chill.

Remove the whisk and the bowl from freezer, and add the cream, sugar, and vanilla. Beat the mixture on medium-high speed for 1 minute, or until it doubles in volume and has stiff peaks. If not using immediately, transfer to an airtight container and store in the refrigerator 8 for 10 hours. When ready to use, whisk for 20 seconds.

BANANA PUDDING

This seasoned recipe makes a comeback every year. It's a solid performer with a dedicated fan club, of which I'm one. Kind of like Jerry Seinfeld, this pudding pleases a lot of people. SERVES 6 TO 8

½ cup sugar

¼ teaspoon kosher salt

3 tablespoons cornstarch

3 egg yolks

2½ cups whole milk

1 whole vanilla bean pod, split,
    seeds scraped from the
    pod, and pod discarded

1 teaspoon butter

1 teaspoon banana extract

1 pint heavy whipping cream

¼ cup powdered sugar

3 medium bananas, cut into slices

1 (11-ounce) box Nilla Wafers

In a double boiler, combine the sugar, salt, and cornstarch, mixing with a balloon whisk until well combined. Add the egg yolks and whisk until all the ingredients are incorporated. Stir in the milk and the vanilla seeds scraped from the pod.

Place the double boiler over medium-high heat and whisk the pudding continuously for 12 to 15 minutes, until thickened.

Turn off the heat and stir in the butter and banana extract. Set aside to rest for 5 minutes–the pudding will continue to thicken as it cools.

Transfer the pudding to a glass bowl and cover with plastic wrap by pressing the wrap directly onto the surface of the pudding. This will prevent a film from forming. Refrigerate until ready to serve.

Meanwhile, place the bowl of a stand mixer and the whisk attachment in the freezer to chill for 15 minutes. Once chilled, combine the whipping cream and sugar in the bowl and whisk just until stiff peaks form. Store the whipped cream in an airtight container until ready to use, or for up to 8 hours. When ready to use, whisk for 20 seconds.

Build the dessert in a large glass bowl by creating 6 layers, alternating the pudding, banana slices, and Nilla wafers. Top with the freshly whipped cream.

CHEESECAKE FLAN

I was living in Mobile, Alabama, at the time I created this recipe, and I discovered that the city has Spanish roots dating back as far as the early 1500s. So I used a Spanish technique of making flan, which I used with cream cheese and eggs to make a lighter, more delicate cheesecake. And the crumble becomes the topping, instead of the crust. SERVES 8

CRUMBLE

1 cup all-purpose flour

1/2 cup brown sugar

1/2 teaspoon baking powder

1/2 teaspoon ground cinnamon

1/2 teaspoon allspice

1/4 teaspoon kosher salt

1/2 cup (1 stick) unsalted butter, at room temperature

3/4 cup old-fashioned oats

FLAN

5 cups whole milk

1 teaspoon cardamom

28 ounces sweetened condensed milk

16 ounces cream cheese, softened

5 large eggs, at room temperature

1 tablespoon vanilla paste or 2 tablespoons vanilla extract

1 teaspoon ground cinnamon

1/8 teaspoon kosher salt

TOPPING

Blueberry sauce, of choice, for garnish

To prepare the crumble, preheat the oven to 375 degrees F. Line a baking sheet with parchment paper.

Whisk the flour, brown sugar, baking powder, cinnamon, allspice, and salt together in a large bowl. Add the butter and work it into the dry mixture with your fingertips, until pea-size lumps form.

Add the oats and mix with your fingertips until clumps form. It should look like crumb topping. Refrigerate for 15 minutes.

Transfer the cooled crumble to the baking sheet and bake for 8 minutes. Using a metal spatula, stir and toss the crumble. Rotate the tray and continue to bake for 8 more minutes, until the crumble is dark golden brown.

Store the crumble in the refrigerator until ready to use.

To prepare the flan, reduce the oven temperature to 350 degrees F.

Bring the milk and cardamom just to a simmer in a heavy saucepan over medium heat. Set aside.

Combine the condensed milk and cream cheese in a food processor and process until smooth. Add the eggs, vanilla, cinnamon, and salt and process until smooth. Transfer to a large bowl and whisk in the hot milk mixture.

Lay out 8 ramekins in a baking pan with high sides. Divide the flan mixture among the ramekins. Add enough hot water to the pan to reach halfway up the side of the ramekins. Bake for 20 to 25 minutes, until the custards are just set. They should wobble in the middle when tapped. Transfer the ramekins to the fridge to cool.

When ready to serve, spoon some of the crumble on top of each ramekin. For a fancier presentation, you can remove the flan from the ramekins, place on individual serving plates, top with blueberry sauce, and then spoon some of the crumble over the top.

CITRUS BREAD PUDDING

This was another one of those dishes that turned out better than I thought it would, and I believe it is because of the bread that we used. We used kaiser rolls for the burgers and ciabatta for the BLTs at One Flew South, so I cubed the old bread, tossed it in melted butter, and toasted it on a baking sheet. OMG! The flavor that came from the toasted cornmeal on those kaiser rolls sent this simple bread pudding to the next level. SERVES 4 TO 6

BREAD PUDDING

½ cup dried cranberries

Zest and juice of 1 orange plus more orange juice, if needed, to measure ½ cup

2 teaspoons orange liqueur

2 kaiser rolls, cubed into ¼-inch pieces

2 ciabatta rolls, cubed into ¼-inch pieces

6 tablespoons butter, melted, plus softened butter for the baking dish

4 cups whole milk

¾ cup sugar, divided

6 whole eggs, beaten

1 egg yolk, beaten

1 whole vanilla bean pod, split, seeds scraped from the pod, and pod discarded

½ teaspoon ground cinnamon

½ teaspoon kosher salt

Preheat the oven to 325 degrees F.

To prepare the bread pudding, combine the dried cranberries, orange juice, and orange liqueur in a bowl and let soak for at least 20 minutes.

Place the kaiser roll and ciabatta bread cubes into a large stainless-steel bowl, drizzle with the melted butter, and toss to combine. Transfer the bread cubes to a baking sheet and bake for 8 to 10 minutes, until light brown.

In a large saucepan, combine the milk, half of the sugar, and the orange zest and bring to a boil over medium-high heat. Turn off the heat.

To make the custard, blend the eggs, egg yolk, vanilla seeds, cinnamon, salt, and the remaining sugar together in a large bowl with a whisk. Temper by gradually adding one-third of the hot milk to the egg mixture, whisking constantly. Add the remaining hot milk, mixing well, then strain the mixture through a fine-mesh sieve into a separate large bowl.

Drain the cranberries, discarding the liquid.

Add the toasted bread and the drained cranberries to the custard, gently mix, and let this soak for at least 1 hour to allow the bread to absorb the custard.

Lightly coat the inside of a 9 x 13-inch glass baking dish with softened butter. Pour the bread pudding mixture into the baking dish and place it into a larger baking pan. Place in the oven and add enough water to the baking pan to go halfway up the baking dish. Bake in the water bath for 1 hour to 1 hour 15 minutes, until the custard is completely set.

ORANGE-BOURBON SAUCE

2 cups freshly squeezed orange juice

½ cup bourbon

½ cup brown sugar

1 whole vanilla bean pod, split, seeds scraped from the pod, and pod discarded

2 tablespoons cornstarch

2 tablespoons water

To make the sauce, in a medium saucepan over medium-high heat, combine the orange juice, bourbon, brown sugar, and vanilla seeds scraped from the pod. Cook until the brown sugar is dissolved and the liquid comes to a boil.

In a small bowl, combine the cornstarch and water to make a smooth slurry. Add the slurry to the saucepan and stir well until the sauce thickens enough to coat the back of a spoon.

Serve the warm bread pudding in small bowls, with the sauce spooned over the top.

"NOT UPSIDE DOWN" CAKE WITH BRAISED PINEAPPLE AND BOURBON SAUCE

This was one of those dishes born out of lack of space, pans, and ovens at the airport. This is a pineapple upside-down cake's kissing cousin! It's a delicious recipe that you don't need to turn upside down to get the same taste. Cooking the pineapple separately and using the liquid as a sauce for the cake after it's baked is the secret. Pass the extra sauce around the table or use it on your waffles for breakfast. MAKES 2 (9-INCH) LOAF CAKES

CAKE

2 tablespoons butter, softened, for the pans

3½ cups all-purpose flour, plus more for the pans

1 (15-ounce) can pumpkin purée

4 large eggs

1 cup vegetable oil

2 cups brown sugar

2 teaspoons baking soda

1½ teaspoons kosher salt

1 teaspoon ground cinnamon

1 teaspoon ground nutmeg

½ teaspoon ground cloves

¼ teaspoon ground ginger

Fresh mint, cut into chiffonade, as garnish

Preheat the oven to 350 degrees F. Grease and flour 2 (9-inch) loaf pans.

To prepare the cake, in a large bowl, combine the pumpkin, eggs, oil, brown sugar, and ⅔ cup water and mix well.

In a separate large bowl, whisk together the 3½ cups flour, baking soda, salt, cinnamon, nutmeg, cloves, and ginger until well blended.

Stir the dry ingredients into the pumpkin mixture and mix until just blended. Equally divide the mixture between the prepared pans and bake for 50 minutes, or until a toothpick inserted in the center comes out clean. Place the pan on a wire rack to cool.

When completely cooled, run a sharp knife around the edge to loosen the cake, then turn it out onto a plate or serving dish.

continued ➝

BRAISED PINEAPPLE AND BOURBON SAUCE

1 fresh pineapple, peeled, cored, and quartered

1/2 cup brown sugar

1/2 cup bourbon

2 cups pineapple juice

1 whole vanilla bean pod, split, seeds scraped from the pod, and pod discarded

2 tablespoons cornstarch

WHIPPED CREAM

1 pint heavy whipping cream

1/4 cup powdered sugar

To prepare the pineapple and bourbon sauce, reduce the oven temperature to 325 degrees F. Place the quartered pineapples in a large baking dish.

In a medium bowl, whisk together the brown sugar, bourbon, and pineapple juice. Pour the mixture over the quartered pineapple in the baking dish. Add the vanilla seeds scraped from the pod and cover the pan with aluminum foil. Bake for 40 minutes, or until the pineapple is fork tender. Set aside to cool.

Transfer the cooled pineapple quarters to a cutting board and cut into chunks. Transfer the pineapple liquid to a small saucepan and bring to boil over medium-high heat.

In a small bowl, combine the cornstarch with 2 tablespoons of water to make a slurry. Add the slurry to the liquid in the saucepan and stir until the sauce slightly thickens.

To prepare the whipped cream, place the bowl from a stand mixer and the whisk attachment in the freezer to chill for 15 minutes.

Combine the whipping cream and sugar in the bowl and whisk just until stiff peaks form. The whipped cream can be stored in an airtight container in the fridge for up to 8 hours. When ready to use, whisk for 20 seconds.

To serve, cut the cake into 1¼-inch-thick slices. In a cast-iron pan over medium-high heat, cook the cakes slices for 2 minutes per side, until slightly charred.

Arrange the cake slices on a serving dish or individual plate and top with the braised pineapple, bourbon sauce, and whipped cream. Garnish with the mint.

ALMOND CAKE AND BASIL-POACHED PEARS WITH BROWN SUGAR– CARAMEL WHIPPED CREAM

Use Bosc pears for this recipe, because they are hard and perfect for poaching. A regular soft green pear will turn to mush. Using cane syrup in the cake instead of sugar results in a dark brown color, and it has a milder sweetness. SERVES 12

BROWN SUGAR– CARAMEL WHIPPED CREAM

¾ teaspoon gelatin powder

2 cups heavy cream

1 vanilla pod, split, or
   1 tablespoon vanilla paste

4 tablespoons brown sugar

⅛ teaspoon kosher salt

BASIL POACHED PEARS

1 cup sugar

¼ cup honey

1 cinnamon stick

10 fresh basil leaves

Juice of 1 lemon

3 Bosc pears, peeled

To prepare the whipped cream, combine the gelatin powder with 1 tablespoon water in a bowl and set aside to bloom.

In a small pot over medium heat, heat the cream with the split vanilla pod until hot, but not boiling. Remove the split vanilla pod and set aside.

In a small saucepan make a "dry caramel" by cooking the brown sugar for about 1 minute, stirring constantly with a high-heat spatula, until smooth and you've built a little flavor.

Pour the hot vanilla cream over the melted brown sugar and whisk over medium heat for about 1 minute, until well combined. Add the bloomed gelatin and salt to the hot mixture and blend with an immersion blender until the gelatin is well incorporated. Then cover and refrigerate for 6 hours.

When you are ready to serve, using a stand mixer, whisk the mixture until medium peaks form.

To prepare the pears, in a medium saucepan, combine the sugar, honey, cinnamon stick, basil, lemon juice, and 2½ cups water and cook over medium heat until the sugar dissolves.

Add the pears to the saucepan, reduce the heat to low, and simmer for 25 minutes, or until the pears are soft and a knife goes easily go in and out of the pears. Set aside.

continued ◄

ALMOND CAKE

1 tablespoon butter,
    softened, for the pan

2 cups almond flour

1 teaspoon baking soda

½ teaspoon kosher salt

2 teaspoons vanilla extract

1 teaspoon almond extract

½ cup Steen's cane syrup

4 large eggs, at room temperature

1 tablespoon grated lemon zest

¼ cup sliced almonds

¼ cup powdered sugar

To prepare the cake, preheat the oven to 350 degrees F. Grease the bottom and sides of a 9-inch cake pan or springform pan. You could also line the bottom of the pan with parchment paper for easy cake removal from pan.

In a large bowl, whisk together the almond flour, baking soda, and salt.

In a medium bowl, whisk together the vanilla extract, almond extract, cane syrup, eggs, and lemon zest. Pour the wet ingredients into the dry ingredients and stir together until combined.

Pour the batter into the greased pan and top with the sliced almonds. Bake for 30 minutes, or until a toothpick in the middle comes out clean. Let cool for 15 to 20 minutes in the pan, then remove the cake from the pan and let cool completely on a wire rack.

Place the cake on a platter and dust with the powdered sugar. Serve with the pears and whipped cream for dessert. The cake with just the powdered sugar makes a lovely treat with your afternoon tea.

CITRUS POUND CAKE WITH BUTTERMILK AND BOURBON

I really hope you enjoy this cake. I made it a million different times before I settled on the final recipe. The bourbon flavor, combined with the buttermilk, gives it a special zip. Buttermilk and Honey Ice Cream (page 209) is a great accompaniment as are the Bourbon and Orange Mixed Berries (page 186) and whipped cream (see page 186). I use a bread loaf pan for this cake, but if you don't have that size, use 2 loaf pans. MAKES 1 (16-INCH) BREAD LOAF PAN OR 2 (8-INCH) LOAF PANS

1 teaspoon oil for the loaf pan

3 cups sugar plus 1 tablespoon for the loaf pan

1½ cups (3 sticks) butter, softened

6 large eggs, at room temperature

3 cups all-purpose flour

½ teaspoon baking powder

½ teaspoon baking soda

¼ teaspoon kosher salt

1 teaspoon vanilla extract

2 teaspoons ground ginger

Zest and juice of 1 lemon

Juice and zest of 1 orange

1 cup buttermilk

5 tablespoons bourbon

Preheat the oven to 325 F. Grease the loaf pan with the oil and dust with 1 table-spoon sugar.

In a stand mixer set on medium speed, mix the 3 cups sugar and butter until light and fluffy. Add the eggs, one at a time, beating just until the yellow disappears.

In a large bowl, sift together the flour, baking powder, baking soda, and salt.

With the mixer off, add the vanilla, ginger, lemon zest and juice, and orange zest and juice. Then add the buttermilk, bourbon, and the flour mixture. Start the mixer on low speed and beat just until the flour is incorporated. Then scrape the sides of the mixer bowl down, and continue to mix on medium speed for 5 minutes, until smooth and creamy.

Pour the cake batter into the prepared pan and bake for 1 hour and 15 minutes. The cake is done when a toothpick placed in the center of the cake comes out clean. Let the cake cool completely in the pan on a wire rack before removing. To remove, run a sharp knife around the edge and turn out onto a plate.

Slice to serve, plain or with any topping you choose.

CHOCOLATE CAKE WITH CREAM CHEESE-WHITE CHOCOLATE FROSTING

At One Flew South, we didn't have room for a mixer so we had to come up with a cake we could make without one. (That said, if you have a mixer, you can certainly use it for this cake.) This recipe also is great for cupcakes. SERVES 8

CHOCOLATE CAKE

1 tablespoon butter, softened, for the pan

1¾ cups sugar, plus 2 tablespoons for dusting the pans

1¾ cups all-purpose flour

¾ cup unsweetened Condor cocoa powder or cocoa powder of choice

1 teaspoon baking powder

2 teaspoons baking soda

1 teaspoon kosher salt

1 teaspoon ground cinnamon

1 teaspoon ground ginger

1 cup buttermilk

¾ cup vegetable oil

2 large eggs, at room temperature

1½ teaspoons vanilla extract

1 cup freshly brewed hot coffee

FROSTING

11 ounces white chocolate, coarsely chopped

1 pound cream cheese, softened

1 tablespoon sour cream

½ cup (1 stick) unsalted butter, softened

1 cup powdered sugar

1 teaspoon vanilla extract

Preheat the oven to 350 degrees F. Butter 2 (8-inch) round cake pans and line the bottoms with parchment paper. Dust the pans with 2 tablespoons sugar.

To make the cake, in a large bowl, sift together the flour, the remaining 1¾ cups sugar, the cocoa powder, baking powder, baking soda, salt, cinnamon, and ginger.

In another bowl, combine the buttermilk, oil, eggs, vanilla, and hot coffee. Add the dry ingredients to the wet ingredients and whisk together until smooth. (Or use a stand mixer with the paddle attachment.)

Divide the batter equally between the prepared cake pans and bake for 30 to 40 minutes, or until a toothpick placed in the center of the cake comes out clean. Let the cakes cool completely in the pans on a wire rack. To remove, run a sharp knife around the edges and turn out onto a plate.

To make the frosting, melt the white chocolate in a double boiler over medium heat, stirring occasionally to make sure the chocolate doesn't get too hot. It should be warm to the touch.

In the bowl of a stand mixer with the paddle attachment, beat the cream cheese, sour cream, butter, and powdered sugar on low speed, slowly increasing the speed, for 4 minutes. Scrape down the sides of the bowl, add the warm melted white chocolate and vanilla and beat for 1 to 2 minutes to incorporate.

To frost the cake, place 1 cake round on a serving plate and spread about ⅓ of the frosting over the top, all the way to the edges of the cake. Place the second cake round on top of the first, and frost the top and sides with the remaining frosting.

FRIED APPLE HAND PIES

Good hot or cold, these little pies are quicker to make than a traditional apple pie—and they travel well. You can also freeze them before you cook them—just let them sit out for 10 minutes to thaw a little and then drop them in the fryer when you're ready to roll—so they make a great dessert to prepare ahead. MAKES 8 TO 10

CINNAMON SUGAR

⅓ cup sugar

1 teaspoon ground cinnamon

⅛ teaspoon ground nutmeg

⅛ teaspoon ground ginger

PIE DOUGH

3 cups all-purpose flour

2 tablespoons sugar

1 teaspoon kosher salt

½ cup (1 stick) cold unsalted butter, cut into cubes

½ cup cold vegetable shortening

6 tablespoons ice water

1 teaspoon apple cider vinegar

To make the cinnamon sugar, whisk together the sugar, cinnamon, nutmeg, and ginger in a small bowl. Set aside.

To make the dough, combine the flour, sugar, and salt in a food processor and pulse to combine. Add the butter and shortening and pulse until the mixture looks like breadcrumbs. Add the ice water and the vinegar, 1 tablespoon at a time, and pulse until the mixture just comes together.

Turn the dough out onto a large piece of plastic wrap and press it into a disc. Wrap it tightly in the plastic wrap and refrigerate for at least 1 hour.

continued ▸

PIE FILLING

2 Granny Smith apples, peeled, cored, and cut into 1/2-inch chunks

2 Gala apples, peeled, cored, and cut into 1/2-inch chunks

1/4 cup packed brown sugar

1/4 cup sugar

1/2 teaspoon ground cinnamon

1/2 teaspoon ground ginger

1/4 teaspoon ground nutmeg

1/4 teaspoon kosher salt

2 teaspoons lemon juice

1 1/2 teaspoons cornstarch

ASSEMBLE AND FRY

3 cups canola oil

1 large egg

To make the filling, combine the apples, brown sugar, sugar, cinnamon, ginger, nutmeg, salt, and lemon juice in a medium saucepan over medium heat, and cook, stirring often, for 5 minutes, until the sugar dissolves and the apples have softened. Stir in the cornstarch, increase the heat, and bring to a boil. When the mixture starts to thicken, remove the pan from the heat. Transfer the filling to a lidded container and let cool to room temperature. Put on the lid and refrigerate until ready to assemble the pie.

To assemble and fry the pies, remove the dough from the fridge and let it come to room temperature.

Pour the oil into a Dutch oven over medium heat, and heat to 365 degrees F. Line a large plate with paper towels and set aside.

On a lightly floured work surface, roll out the dough to 1/8 inch thick. Cut out 4 1/2-inch circles. Gather the extra dough pieces, reroll, and keep cutting. You will need 8 to 10 circles.

Beat the egg with 1 tablespoon water in a small bowl to make an egg wash.

Place about 1 heaping tablespoon of the apple filling into the center of each dough round. Brush the edges with the egg wash and then fold the dough over to make a half-moon shape. Gently press out the air with your hand and seal the edges of the dough with a fork. Repeat with the remaining filling and dough.

Place 4 to 6 pies at a time into the hot oil in the Dutch oven and cook for 5 minutes, flipping as needed, until they are golden brown overall. Transfer the pies to the paper towel-lined plate to drain.

Sprinkle the cinnamon sugar over the warm pies. Serve warm or at room temperature.

Buttermilk and Honey Ice Cream (page 209)

OATMEAL CHOCOLATE CHIP COOKIES

I'll admit it: I'm a cookie monster and I wish I didn't love this recipe so much. I'm tired of having cookie crumbs in bed while I watch TV. MAKES 20 COOKIES

1 cup (2 sticks) unsalted butter, softened

1 cup packed brown sugar

½ cup sugar

1 egg, at room temperature

1 egg yolk, at room temperature

1 tablespoon vanilla extract

2 cups all-purpose flour

1 teaspoon baking powder

1 teaspoon baking soda

1 cup old fashioned oats

1 teaspoon kosher salt

2½ cups semisweet chocolate chips

Preheat the oven to 325 degrees F. Line one or two baking sheets with parchment paper, or lightly spray them with vegetable oil.

Using a stand mixer with the paddle attachment, cream together the butter and the sugars, until smooth. Add the egg, egg yolk, and vanilla and mix until incorporated.

In a separate bowl, whisk together the flour, baking powder, baking soda, oats, and salt. With the mixer off, add the flour mixture to the butter-egg mixture, and mix with a spoon until incorporated. Scrape the bottom and sides of the bowl, and pulse briefly just to incorporate everything. Stir in the chocolate chips.

Using a ¼-cup muffin scoop, scoop the dough onto the prepared baking sheets, leaving 1½ to 2 inches of space between the cookies. Bake for 12 to 17 minutes, until the cookies have a slightly dark edge and a soft middle, or to your desired degree of doneness.

Transfer the cookies to a wire rack and let cool. These cookies can be stored in an airtight container for up to 1 week.

RED WINE–POACHED PEARS WITH HONEY-MASCARPONE AND SPICED PECANS

Don't be fooled by the title, this is a deceptively simple recipe, and quick to prepare. But it is rich and decadent, nonetheless. You can mix up the mascarpone ahead and refrigerate it, then prepare the rest of the recipe just before serving. Use a Bosc pear, which is a firmer variety and holds up to poaching. You can make this dessert using firm, fresh plums as well, just cook them for less time. SERVES 8

HONEY MASCARPONE

2 cups mascarpone cheese

¼ cup honey

1 teaspoon ground ginger

Zest of 1 orange

Zest of 1 lemon

PEARS

4 Bosc pears, peeled, halved and cored

Zest and juice of 2 lemons, with the juice of 1 lemon set aside

1½ cups red wine (I like zinfandel or merlot for this)

¾ cup sugar

2 teaspoons vanilla extract

3 star anise pods

1 cinnamon stick or 1 teaspoon ground cinnamon

Spiced Pecans (page 79)

To prepare the mascarpone, in a medium bowl, combine the mascarpone, honey, ginger, orange zest, and lemon zest and mix with a spoon or spatula until smooth. For an airier, whipped spread, mix with an immersion blender. Cover and chill for at least 3 hours before using.

To prepare the pears, place the pears in a bowl and add just enough water to cover them. Add the juice of 1 lemon to the water to prevent browning. Set aside.

Place a wire rack over paper towels.

In a medium pot, combine the red wine, sugar, vanilla, star anise, cinnamon stick, zest, and the juice from other lemon. (There should be about 1 inch of liquid in the pot.) Bring the mixture to a boil over high heat. Reduce the heat to maintain a simmer and add the pears. Simmer for 12 to 15 minutes on one side, then flip over the pears and continue to poach another 8 to 10 minutes, or until they are fork tender. Carefully remove the pears from the pot and transfer to the rack to cool.

Bring the liquid in the pot to a boil and cook until it is reduced by half.

Serve the pears at room temperature in shallow bowls, drizzled with the reduced wine sauce, dolloped with honey-mascarpone, and sprinkled with Spiced Pecans.

GRILLED PEACHES WITH SPICED WHIPPED CREAM

This is an item that can be savory or sweet. To make it savory, simply grill the peaches without the sugar mixture and leave off the whipped cream. Garnish with some toasted pecans and mint.

SERVES 4 TO 6

SPICED WHIPPED CREAM

½ cup heavy cream

½ teaspoon vanilla extract

1 tablespoon powdered sugar

¼ teaspoon ground cardamom

¼ teaspoon ground ginger

2 tablespoons sour cream

GRILLED PEACHES

¼ cup brown sugar

½ teaspoon ground ginger

½ teaspoon ground cinnamon

⅛ teaspoon ground nutmeg

4 ripe peaches, halved and pitted

1 tablespoon extra-virgin olive oil

To make the whipped cream, in a large bowl, combine the heavy cream, vanilla, sugar, cardamom, and ginger. Using a stand mixer or a large balloon whisk, whisk the cream until soft peaks form. Add the sour cream and whisk to medium peaks. Refrigerate until ready to use.

To grill the peaches, preheat a grill or a grill pan over medium-high heat.

In a small bowl, stir together the brown sugar, ginger, cinnamon, and nutmeg. Set aside.

Brush the cut sides of the halved peaches with oil. Place them cut-side down on the grill and brush the tops with the remaining oil.

Grill for 4 to 6 minutes, or until grill marks start to form and the peaches begin to soften. Carefully flip the peaches and sprinkle them with the brown sugar mixture. Grill for additional 3 to 5 minutes, or until the brown sugar has melted and the peaches are soft.

Transfer the peaches to a platter or individual bowls. Serve with dollops of spiced whipped cream.

CHOCOLATE-COFFEE SEMIFREDDO WITH RASPBERRIES AND TOASTED PECANS

Although the literal interpretation of the Italian "semifreddo" means half-frozen, this dessert is actually fully frozen—but never fear, it melts in your mouth. SERVES 8

1 teaspoon vegetable oil, for the loaf pan

1½ cups heavy cream

1 tablespoon instant coffee powder

1½ tablespoons unsweetened cocoa powder, divided

1 tablespoon bourbon

½ teaspoon vanilla extract

4 large eggs

½ cup sugar

¾ cup pecan pieces, toasted in a dry pan for 3 minutes

8 ounces raspberries

Lightly oil a 9-inch loaf pan and line the pan with plastic wrap, making sure there is enough overhang so you can lift the semifreddo out of the pan later. (The oil helps the plastic wrap slide out easier after it's frozen.)

With a stand mixer, whisk the cream to soft peaks, just until it holds its shape. Set aside.

In a double boiler, combine the coffee powder, 1 tablespoon cocoa powder, bourbon, vanilla, eggs, and sugar and cook, whisking constantly, for 2 to 3 minutes, until the sugar and instant coffee dissolve and the custard thickens enough to coat the back of a spoon.

Set aside to cool to room temperature. When the mixture is cool, fold the whipped cream into the coffee mixture until fully incorporated. Pour the mixture into the loaf pan, cover with the plastic wrap, and freeze overnight.

When you are ready to serve, carefully unwrap the top of the pan. Invert a serving dish over the pan and, holding the dish and pan together, quickly turn it over so the serving dish is on the bottom. Carefully lift off the pan. The semifreddo should come right out. Remove the plastic wrap.

To serve, dust with the remaining ½ tablespoon cocoa powder, and top with the toasted pecans and raspberries. Cut into slices.

BUTTERMILK AND HONEY ICE CREAM

You could make plain vanilla ice cream again, but why, when you can make buttermilk ice cream? The buttermilk adds something of a tangy lemony flavor after it warms a little in your bowl. It's a great change of pace. This base is best made the day before you churn the ice cream. This is perfect served with the Fried Apple Hand Pies (page 201).

Because the buttermilk adds water to the recipe, I use a lot more egg yolks than standard as the added fat reduces the amount of ice crystals in the ice cream. This version is thicker and creamier than most ice cream. You can save the egg whites for another recipe. I like to scramble them and have them on toast for a low-fat breakfast. MAKES 2 QUARTS

4 cups heavy cream

2 cups sugar, divided

2 whole vanilla bean pods, split, seeds scraped from the pods, and pod discarded

½ cups honey

Zest of 2 lemons

24 large egg yolks

4 cups cold buttermilk

Pinch of salt

In a large, heavy saucepan, combine the cream, 1 cup sugar, the vanilla seeds scraped from the pods, honey, and lemon zest and bring to a simmer over medium heat.

In a large bowl, whisk together the egg yolks and the remaining 1 cup of sugar.

Remove the cream mixture from the heat and slowly drizzle a small amount over the yolks, whisking constantly to keep the eggs from curdling. Do this a few more times to warm up the yolks before pouring the yolk mixture into the hot cream, whisking constantly.

Return the tempered mixture to the saucepan on low heat and whisk constantly for 10 to 15 minutes, until the mixture is thick enough to coat the back of a spoon. Strain the mixture through a fine-mesh strainer into a bowl, discard the lemon zest, and set custard aside to cool slightly.

When cooled slightly, whisk in the buttermilk and salt. Let cool to room temperature. Cover and refrigerate overnight for the best flavor and texture.

The next day, freeze in an ice cream maker according to the manufacturer's directions.

COFFEE ICE CREAM

If you have to have your coffee before you go to sleep, this is the way to go. You can substitute decaf for the regular coffee called for in this recipe if you like. Be sure to start this recipe the day before you plan to serve it because the base needs to be refrigerated overnight. MAKES 2 QUARTS

2 cups heavy cream, divided

1 cup whole milk

1 cup sugar

¼ teaspoon salt

6 egg yolks

2 teaspoons vanilla extract

½ cup strong-brewed hot coffee

Fill a large bowl with ice and water, set another bowl on top, and set a fine-mesh strainer in the bowl.

In a medium saucepan, combine the cream, milk, sugar, and salt and cook over medium heat, stirring frequently, just until the sugar dissolves. When the liquid is steamy, but not boiling, remove from the heat.

In a medium bowl, whisk together the egg yolks and vanilla.

Slowly pour ¼ cup of the warm cream mixture into the yolks, whisking constantly, to temper the eggs.

Transfer the warm egg mixture to the pot with the remaining cream mixture, and whisk to combine. Return the pot to medium heat, stirring frequently with a rubber spatula and scraping the bottom and the sides of the pot, until the mixture is thick enough to coat the back of a spoon.

Immediately pour the mixture through a fine-mesh strainer into the large bowl over ice, stir, and let the ice-filled bowl underneath cool the ice cream to room temperature.

Remove the bowl from the ice water, add the hot coffee, and stir again until the mixture comes to room temperature. Cover, and refrigerate the ice cream base overnight.

The next day, pour the mixture in your ice cream maker and churn according to the manufacturer's instructions.

COFFEE-FLUFF MILKSHAKE

My love for the Nutter Butter cookie goes back before my mom got married and I became a Nutter. With that being said, you will understand why there's always a Nutter-Butter-something on my menus. This recipe calls for only five cookies but don't worry, you can enjoy the rest of the package anytime! Marshmallow crème is available at most grocery stores. MAKES 2 SMALL SHAKES (OR IF YOU'RE MY SIZE, 1 LARGE SHAKE)

2 cups Coffee Ice Cream (page 211)

3 tablespoons Marshmallow Fluff

¼ cup milk

6 Nutter Butter cookies, divided

2 tablespoons creamy peanut butter

Whipped cream (see page 186), optional, for topping

Sprinkles, for topping

Combine the ice cream, 2 tablespoons marshmallow crème, milk, 4 Nutter Butter cookies, and peanut butter in a blender and purée on medium speed until smooth and creamy.

Pour the shake into 2 glasses, top with a dollop of the remaining marshmallow crème, some whipped cream, if using, and an additional Nutter Butter cookie to top it off if you wish, and some sprinkles.

ACKNOWLEDGMENTS

I have to start by thanking my mom. Without her I would neither be here nor have the confidence to write this book.

I would like to thank all my friends who put up with me through this process: Tiannne, for letting me bounce recipe ideas off her, and giving me real home cook feedback. Kari, my hardcore home-steading friend, who sent me sourdough starters to play with. My good friend Michael Jenkins, for always making sure we don't give up on our dreams. (I finished writing this book just before he started his—keep pushing, Mike, your turn is next.) My business partner Reggie Washington, for putting up with my dozing off in financial meetings because I was up all night long typing recipes and headnotes.

I would like to send a big thanks to my team who helped put this dream together: Annette Joseph, my food stylist (I'll be looking forward to my next trip to Italy, I'm giving you a call), my photographer, Deborah Whitlaw Llewellyn, and my two chefs, Carlos Granderson and Ken Harmon, for all those last-minute store runs.

Thanks to all the folks at Gibbs Smith for believing in my project.

I would also like to thank my team at Pulse Point marketing, and all the good folks at Gumbo Marketing, including Panda!

Having an idea and turning it into a book is as hard as it sounds. The experience was often grueling, and I don't think I could have done it without a key person who held me together, and who I now consider a friend—Janice Shay of Pinafore Press. She kept this train on the track. When the tree fell on my house, I was in a bad place. Then I had foot surgery and had to learn how to walk again. Through it all, Janice told me, "You're not going to give up, not while I still know how to type." I can't thank her enough!

INDEX

METRIC CONVERSION CHART

VOLUME MEASUREMENTS		WEIGHT MEASUREMENTS		TEMPERATURE CONVERSION	
U.S.	Metric	U.S.	Metric	Fahrenheit	Celsius
1 teaspoon	5 ml	½ ounce	15 g	250	120
1 tablespoon	15 ml	1 ounce	30 g	300	150
¼ cup	60 ml	3 ounces	90 g	325	160
⅓ cup	75 ml	4 ounces	115 g	350	180
½ cup	125 ml	8 ounces	225 g	375	190
⅔ cup	150 ml	12 ounces	350 g	400	200
¾ cup	175 ml	1 pound	450 g	425	220
1 cup	250 ml	2¼ pounds	1 kg	450	230

ABOUT THE AUTHOR

Born in Louisiana and raised on Creole and Southern cuisine, **Chef Duane Nutter** began his culinary career in 1994 at the age of twenty, studying under well-respected Chef Darryl Evans at the Four Seasons Hotel in Atlanta.

After splitting his time between the kitchen, and open-mic nights doing stand-up comedy as "The Mad Chef," Nutter was named chef and spokesperson for the National Peanut Board. This job took him on the road for demonstrations and cooking shows, where he honed his considerable sense of humor (he wore a Styrofoam peanut hat during the demonstrations).

Next, Nutter cooked at the Ritz-Carlton in Palm Beach, Florida. In 2004, he moved to Louisville, Kentucky and became chef de cuisine at the Seelbach Hilton's Oakroom, one of only forty-eight AAA Five-Diamond restaurants in the world. His cooking received superb reviews, noting his "complex interpretations of seemingly simple dishes."

In 2006, Nutter was invited to compete on the Food Network's *Iron Chef America*, and in 2007 he cooked at the prestigious James Beard House in New York City. His food has been praised in a variety of highly regarded publications, including *Garden & Gun*, *Men's Journal*, *Delta Sky Magazine*, *Condé Nast Traveler*, *Atlanta Magazine*, and *Details*.

In 2008, with a new vision and challenge in mind, Nutter accepted the position in Atlanta as One Flew South's executive chef. Using his imaginative execution to blend Southern ingredients with world travel influences, he created a menu for the first upscale travel-dining restaurant, at the world's busiest airport. One Flew South was a James Beard semifinalist for Outstanding Service in 2014 and 2015.

In 2017, Nutter opened the Southern National restaurant in Mobile, Alabama, with restaurateur and friend, Reggie Washington. Southern National was a James Beard semifinalist in 2018 for "Best New Restaurant in the South."

Chef Duane was a James Beard nominee for Best New Chef in both 2018 and 2022. Southern National was included in "The Restaurant List: The 50 Places in America We're Most excited about," *New York Times*, 2021.

In 2022, Chef Duane moved back to Atlanta, relocating his Southern National restaurant there in 2023.

In 2024, Southern National was included in "The 25 Best Restaurants in Atlanta Right Now," *New York Times*. The same year, he designed and opened a Southern National Market in the Atlanta airport, in one of its busiest international concourses.